# Studies In Jainism:

## Reader 2

Edited by

Duli Chandra Jain

Jain Study Circle

Editorial Advisors:

| | | |
|---|---|---|
| Vinay K. Vakani | Chandrakant P. Shah | Krishna Kumar Mehta |
| Jayantilal Shah | Ahamindra Jain | Anil & Parnita Jain |
| Sunita Jain | Richa Jain, Rashmi Jain | Rajesh Jain |

Cover:
Interior views of Delwara Jain Temples
Mt. Abu, Rajasthan, India
Photos by DCJ



Library of Congress Catalog Card No. 90 - 091543

ISBN 0 - 9626105 - 2 - 6 Softcover

Published by
Jain Study Circle, Inc.
99-11 60 Avenue, #3D
Flushing, New York, 11368
USA

Printed in the United States of America

Bhagwaan Mahaveer

Dedicated to

**The New Generation Of Jains**

Idol of Bhagwaan Parshvanath
(Tenth Century A. D.)

# Contents

* * * * * * *

I am not in favor of Mahaveer due to faith in him, nor am I against other philosophers like Kapil due to aversion. I am of the opinion that he whose ideas stand true on the scale of logic should be followed.

- Acharya Haribhadra Suri

* * * * * * *

# Preface

These are exciting times for Jainism. For the first time in recorded history, a significant population of Jains is residing outside of India. We are living in the age of science and technology, computers and communication satellites, and rockets and space exploration. All over the world, political and socio-economic systems are undergoing important changes. With the dawn of freedom and democracy, which some of us have personally witnessed, India has made significant progress in the past few decades in various fields, including agriculture, industry and education. Indians who have migrated to North America, including youngsters, have made excellent use of the opportunities presented to them. Jains are no exception.

In India as well as in North America, Jains are playing a significant role in diverse fields and are enjoying the benefits of their endeavors. There has been a significant rise in the level of education in the Jain community. Consequently, Jains have achieved greater awareness and understanding of the basics of religion. They have developed the ability to distinguish between blind faith and rationalism, between myths and reality, and between meaningless rituals and the genuine practice of religion. A healthy dialogue is continuing on the unique features of Jainism. The series 'Studies In Jainism' is an effort to contribute to this dialogue.

The concepts presented in the book conform to the Jain scriptures, which are works of great thinkers and philosophers of the past. Every effort has been made to present the principles of Jainism from a rational viewpoint. The lessons include the concept of reality in Jainism and a presentation of rational perception, rational knowledge and rational conduct for householders. These are based on scriptures and are interspersed with prayers, stories and dialogues. A few scholarly articles appear towards the end of the book.

The code of ethics of all religions, including Jainism, is essentially the same. However, the Jain code of conduct is based on our concepts of universe and of reality. Moreover, Jains practice ethical conduct not because some higher authority commands them to do so. They do not celebrate any worship to please any superhuman or supernatural being. Jains conduct their lives in a rational manner in order to attain happiness and peace of mind individually as well as collectively.

The present book follows Studies In Jainism: Primer and Reader 1. It is the result of the joint effort of a large group of individuals. Most of the material has been adopted from the Jain Study Circular. Thus, the writers of the Jain Study Circular should be given the most credit for their contributions. The editorial advisors have made valuable comments and suggestions. I am also grateful for the advice, encouragement and help given by Ms. Kristin Dervishian, Dr. Jyotiben Gandhi, Dr. Chaman Lal Jain, Dr. T. J. Salgia, Mr. Naresh Shah and other friends.

D. C. J.

* * * * * * *

A person performing penance
with a desire of fame or worship,
who renounces worldly possessions,
even though born rich,
does not achieve a genuine penance;
so penance should be observed
without pomp and show,
and one should not flaunt or praise it.

From SAMAN SUTTAM

* * * * * * *

## NAMOKAAR MANTRA (णमोकार मंत्र)

### REVERENCE MANTRA: A Worship of Virtues

णमो अरिहंताणं

NAMO ARIHANTAANAM

We revere the Supreme Human Beings (ARIHANTs) (because they achieve absolute truth and devote themselves to the uplift of life on earth).

णमो सिद्धाणं

NAMO SIDDHAANAM

We revere the Supreme Beings (SIDDHAs) (because they are souls having absolute perception, knowledge and bliss).

णमो आयरियाणं

NAMO AYARIYAANAM

We revere the sages who preach (ACHARYAs) (because they master the principles of religion).

णमो उवज्झायाणं

NAMO UVAJJHAAYAANAM

We revere the sages who study (UPAADHYAAYAs) (because they engage in enhancing their knowledge of matter and souls).

णमो लोए सव्व साहूणं

NAMO LOAE SAVVA SAAHOONAM

We revere all sages (SADHUs) (because they devote their lives to the selfless pursuit of the enlightenment of all).[1]

(We revere them with a resolve to follow in their footsteps and make our lives more meaningful.)

एसो पंच णमोक्कारो सव्व पावप्पणासणो ।
मंगलाणं च सव्वेसिं पढमं हवइ मंगलं ॥

ESO PANCH NAMOKKAARO SAVVA PAAVAPPANAASANO:
MANGALAANAM CHA SAVVESIM PADHAMAM HAVAI MANGALAM::

This five-fold reverence eliminates all demerit.
It is the first and foremost among all auspiciousness.

---

1 PRAKRIT text is from KALPASUTRA. णमो is also written as नमो. ARIHANT (अरिहंत) is also spelled as ARAHANT (अर्हंत).

## Auspicious Recital (मंगल पाठ)

चत्तारि मंगलं । अरिहंता मंगलं । सिद्धा मंगलं ।
साहू मंगलं । केवलि पण्णत्तो धम्मो मंगलं ।

CHATTARI MANGALAM; ARIHANTA MANGALAM; SIDDHA MANGALAM; SAAHOO MANGALAM; KEVALI PANNATTO DHAMMO MANGALAM

There are four auspicious entities in the universe.
ARIHANTs are auspicious.
SIDDHAs are auspicious.
SADHUs are auspicious.
The religion elucidated by the omniscient is auspicious.

चत्तारि लोगुत्तमा । अरिहंता लोगुत्तमा । सिद्धा लोगुत्तमा ।
साहू लोगुत्तमा । केवलि पण्णत्तो धम्मो लोगुत्तमो ।

CHATTARI LOGUTTAMA; ARIHANTA LOGUTTAMA; SIDDHA LOGUTTAMA; SAAHOO LOGUTTAMA; KEVALI PANNATTO DHAMMO LOGUTTAMO

There are four supreme entities in the universe.
ARIHANTs are supreme.
SIDDHAs are supreme.
SADHUs are supreme.
The religion elucidated by the omniscient is supreme.

चत्तारि सरणं पव्वज्जामि । अरिहंते सरणं पव्वज्जामि ।
सिद्धे सरणं पव्वज्जामि । साहू सरणं पव्वज्जामि ।
केवलि पण्णत्तं धम्मं सरणं पव्वज्जामि ।

CHATTARI SARANAM PAVVAJJAAMI; ARIHANTE SARANAM PAVVAJJAAMI; SIDDHE SARANAM PAVVAJJAAMI; SAAHOO SARANAM PAVVAJJAAMI; KEVALI PANNATTAM DHAMMAM SARANAM PAVVAJJAAMI

I aspire for reliance on four entities of the universe.
I aspire for reliance on ARIHANTs.
I aspire for reliance on SIDDHAs.
I aspire for reliance on SADHUs.
I aspire for reliance on the religion elucidated by the omniscient.

## NAMOKAAR MANTRA: A Unique Worship Of Virtues

Adapted from SAMAN SUTTAM CHAYANIKA[1]

NAMOKAAR Mantra is a worship of the virtues of the five supreme benevolent personalities (PARAMESHTHI): ARIHANTs (Supreme Human Beings), SIDDHAs (Supreme Beings), ACHARYAs (monks who preach), UPAADHYAAYAs (monks who study the scriptures) and SADHUs (monks who indulge in spiritual pursuit).[2] We revere the supreme attributes of these personalities and we aspire for reliance on them. Our reverence and worship entail learning their virtues and instilling them in our lives.

NAMOKAAR Mantra relates to a very important principle of the Jain religion. We Jains worship the virtues of ARIHANTs, SIDDHAs, ACHARYAs, UPAADHYAAYAs and SADHUs. We worship Bhagwaan[3] Mahaveer and other TEERTHANKARs because they have attained rational perception and rational knowledge, and by practicing rational conduct, they epitomized the path to liberation. Worship of virtues entails practicing what we believe in. We can also worship the virtues of other religious personalities such as Bhagwaan Ram, Bhagwaan Krishna, Bhagwaan Buddha, Prophet Mohammed, Guru Nanak and Jesus Christ. However, it should be noted that we do not believe in things that do not conform to our direct observation, knowledge and experience. Thus we do not worship miracles or supernatural phenomena. We believe that no worship, prayer or mantra can alleviate pain and suffering, no person can perform miracles, no religious rites performed by others can help us in our

---

1 SAMAN SUTTAM CHAYANIKA by Dr. Kamal Chand Sogani, former Chairman and Professor of Philosophy, Sukhadia University, Udaipur, published by Prakrit Bharati Academy, Jaipur, 1985; Introduction, pages viii-ix.

2 In Jainism, the five supreme benevolent personalities are represented by the symbol OM (ॐ A A A U M). It is an acronym formed from the Sanskrit words ARIHANT, ASHAREERI (SIDDHAs who do not have material bodies), ACHARYA, UPAADHYAAYA and MUNI (SADHU).

3 The word Bhagwaan essentially means venerable.

material or spiritual pursuit, and no spiritual progress or salvation can be attained by merely accepting a religion or a religious personality such as ARIHANT or SIDDHA. Physical, mental and spiritual well-being can be achieved only through self-endeavor and by imbibing virtues.

**Attribute-based Reverence (GUNAATMAK NAMASKAR)**

We revere the five supreme benevolent personalities, ARIHANTs (Supreme Human Beings), SIDDHAs (Supreme Beings), ACHARYAs (monks who preach), UPAADHYAAYAs (monks who study the scriptures) and SADHUs (monks who indulge in spiritual pursuit). This reverence is impersonal. It is focused on their virtues – good qualities. Indeed, it is a remembrance of their virtues. It is reverence for their virtues. Reverence for virtues promotes a genuine aspiration for them. Although the attributes belong to an individual, the reverence expressed in NAMOKAAR Mantra is for the virtues. An individual becomes celebrated because of his virtuous character. Therefore, it is appropriate to value the virtues of the individual. The endeavor to imbibe the virtues of ARIHANTs, SIDDHAs, ACHARYAs, UPAADHYAAYAs and SADHUs constitutes supreme spiritual pursuit. Thus the expression of reverence for their virtues is the most auspicious prayer.

Attribute-based prayer instills reverence for virtues and by having reverence for virtues, an individual cultivates humanism. The hideous discrimination based on caste, province, nationality, family and appearance is eliminated by imbibing love for virtues. ARIHANTs achieve self-realization, they attain salvation in their lifetime and they show the path to liberation for all. SIDDHAs are free from worldly existence, they do not have material bodies and they experience spiritual bliss. ACHARYAs practice the five major vows: nonviolence, truth, non-stealing, celibacy and non-possessiveness. They are scholars of the various schools of thought. Their experience glows with virtuous conduct and they are beacons on the path to spiritual uplift. Monks have high moral character and are modest. They do not indulge in worldly affairs. We depend on the five supreme benevolent personalities to learn to deal with our ups and downs, trials and tribulations. We wish to instill the virtues of the five supreme benevolent personalities in our lives.

NAMOKAAR Mantra reminds us of this goal. Because of this extremely significant feature, NAMOKAAR Mantra is a unique prayer.

**Attribute-based Reliance (GUNAATMAK SHARAN)**

All of us depend on each other's help. However, this reliance on each other is inadequate for our peace of mind. Therefore, we aspire for reliance on ARIHANTs, SIDDHAs and SADHUs. In their absence, the teachings of those who have attained self-realization are beneficial. So we revere and rely on the teachings of the great souls, who have exemplified the path to liberation. Attribute-based reliance generates virtuous experience. It impels us to pursue a virtuous path. It leads to self-awareness. It is observed that one who follows a virtuous person gradually becomes like that great soul. He/she imbibes the virtues of his/her paragon. When reliance turns into devotion, ego vanishes and one's personality is transformed. Such an individual radiates spiritualism. He is involved in the well-being of all.

NAMOKAAR MANTRA epitomizes these principles and hence it is the most auspicious prayer.

* * * * * * *

NAMOKAAR MANTRA: A Rational View

I wish to concentrate while reciting this mantra. However, the mind wanders while the tongue does its thing. The two are not in harmony. I never recited this mantra in adversity, for overcoming obstacles or for relieving indisposition. These do not relate to the purpose of this mantra.

- Dr. Devendra Kumar Jain

* * * * * * *

# The Eternal Nature Of Jainism

by Dr. Chandrakant P. Shah, Devyani C. Shah and Duli Chandra Jain

According to Jain belief, "Truth exists from time immemorial, and the world, composed of living and non-living substances, has been in existence for all eternity, and undergoes an infinite number of variations, produced simply by the physical and superphysical powers inherent in the substances."[1] A similar observation has been made by Einstein in these words: "Scientific research is based on the idea that everything that takes place is determined by laws of nature, and therefore this holds for the actions of people."[2] The universe has always been in existence. On account of the intrinsic properties of its entities, which include the forces of nature, the universe continually undergoes transformations.

Evidently, the Jain view of the universe precludes the necessity for a Creator. It also affirms that there is no Supreme Being who regulates the events of the world. There is no divine intervention in the lives of worldly beings. No one rewards and punishes us for our deeds. Natural forces govern events such as rain and shine, good crops and famines, and, droughts and floods. These result from the intrinsic attributes of matter and energy. There are no gods to appease. This is the fundamental precept of the culture of the self-reliant (SHRAMANs). B. P. Wadia, a well-known scholar, writes, "Next to the central doctrine of AHIMSA (nonviolence), Jainism facilitates a life of self-exertion because it rejects logically the pernicious belief in an anthropomorphic (having human qualities) personal God. Believers in an extra-cosmic personal God naturally fall into the sin of dependence on such a God, pray to Him, try to propitiate Him and seek favors from Him, thus debasing their moral propensities and their will power."[3]

---

1 An Encyclopedia of Jainism by P. C. Nahar and K. G. Ghosh, Satguru Publications, Delhi, 1988, pages 4-5.
In this quotation, 'world' implies universe.
Superphysical powers are the physical and abstract karma associated with the worldly souls.

2 Albert Einstein: The Human Side by Helen Dukas and Benesh Hoffman, Princeton University Press, Princeton NJ, page 32.

The Jain concept of the universe has no conflict with modern theories of science. The Jain view of the universe implies that intelligent life evolved and possibly became extinct at various places in the universe at various times. Consequently, religious concepts similar to the Jain principles of nonviolence (AHIMSA), rationalism (SAMYAKTVA) and relativism (SYAADAVAAD) must have evolved at various times in the history of the universe. According to this premise, the religion based on these principles is eternal.

SANATAN DHARM, the eternal Indian religion, commonly known as Hinduism, also says that the universe has no beginning and that the principles of religion have been in existence since time immemorial. According to the Vedas, there are three eternal entities: God, nature (PRAKRITI) and soul. Nature evolves and the universe goes through phases of creation and destruction, like sunrise and sunset. God has three aspects, BRAHMA (Creator), VISHNU (Protector) and SHIVA (Destroyer). BRAHMA is responsible for the phase of creation, though the universe is not created out of vacuum. The process of creation is merely a transformation of the existing substance.[4] Each cycle of creation consists of four epochs called SATAYUG, DWAAPAR, TRETA and KALIYUG. Morality and justice among the masses decline gradually with the passage of time, the SATAYUG being the period of highest morality and justice for all and KALIYUG is the period of decline of moral values.

According to Jain belief, each epoch is like a wave, which consists of a crest and a trough. The ascending period is called UTSARPINI while the descending period, AVASARPINI. The ascending and descending periods are each divided into six eras. In the six eras of the ascending period, the moral fabric of individuals and society improves, while in the eras of the descending period, the opposite happens. Twenty-four TEERTHANKARs are born during each period. They reinstate the Jain religious system and modify it according to the needs of the time, without compromising its basic principles. It should be noted that TEERTHANKARs are born as human beings, purify their souls and

3 'Jainism: A Way Of Life' by B. P. Wadia, included in the book 'The Doctrine of Jainism', published by Vallabhsuri Smarak Nidhi, Bombay, 1983, page 61.

4 This is, in particular, the belief of the SAMKHYA school of thought which was expounded by Kapil, one of the great sages of ancient India.

attain the state of eternal bliss (NIRVANA) at the end of their lives. In the present period, which is a descending one, the first TEERTHANKAR was Rishabhadev and the last, Mahaveer. In addition to reinstating the Jain religious system, Bhagwaan Rishabhadev also established the social and economic order. The names of Rishabhadev (Adinath), Ajitnath (the second TEERTHANKAR) and Arishtanemi (the twenty-second TEERTHANKAR) are mentioned with reverence in the YAJURVEDA. Most scholars accept that Parshvanath, the twenty-third TEERTHANKAR, who was born in 949 B.C. and attained NIRVANA in 849 B.C., was a historical personality. Bhagwaan Mahaveer, the last TEERTHANKAR of this period, who was a contemporary of Bhagwaan Buddha, lived from 599 B.C. to 527 B.C.

In conclusion, the Jain religion was not founded by any individual. It has no beginning and no end. Jainism, with its universal principles of nonviolence (AHIMSA), rationalism (SAMYAKTVA) and relativism (SYAADAVAAD) is eternal.

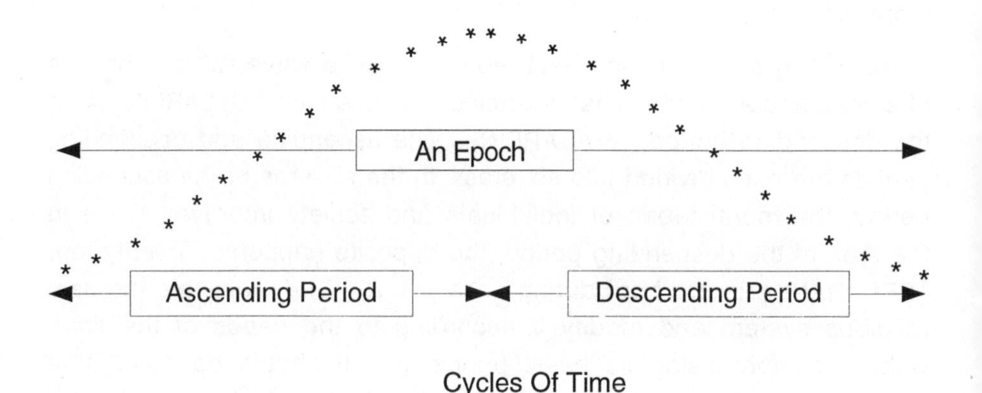


Cycles Of Time

# Basis For Ethics In Jainism

by Dr. Kokila P. Doshi

What is the ultimate purpose of human life? Is it spiritual uplift? How does one reach this spiritual goal? What are the obstacles in the path? What are the solutions?

All religions address these basic questions. Thus there is a fundamental unity of purpose among all religions. But the way these questions are answered reflects the diversity and uniqueness of each religion.

According to Jainism, *influx of karmic matter is the cause of births and rebirths. Stoppage of that influx and shedding of accumulated karmic matter lead to liberation.* It is this tenet that forms the basis of Jain philosophy and Jain ethics.

## The Philosophy: Nine Fundamentals

Jainism believes that the universe is everlasting. It has no beginning or end. There are two kinds of entities in the universe: Living beings (JEEVS) and non-living substances (AJEEVS). The non-living entities are matter (including energy), principle of motion, principle of rest, space and time. Souls comprise the living entity. It is the association of soul and (karmic) matter that is at the root of the cycle of birth and rebirth, causing the suffering of the worldly souls. Salvation (MOKSHA) is the dissolution of this association. The aim of human life is to annihilate the bondage of karmic matter and thus purify the soul. A soul achieves this goal in stages - in a number of reincarnations.

Soul in its innate form is pure, possessing infinite consciousness, knowledge and bliss. However, the veil of karmic matter eclipses its true nature. The soul of a living being receives karma particles in everyday life, through the actions of mind, speech and body, as shown in the schematic chart below. The influx (ASHRAV) of karmic particles leads to misery and suffering. Unlike some other religions, Jainism believes that karmas are not just symbolic expressions of good or bad deeds but they are material particles that get attached to the soul and obstruct the soul's spiritual uplift.

The concept of karma, its relationship to worldly souls and the process of salvation can be explained by an analogy. Imagine a person on the bank of a river, wanting to cross the river in his boat. He starts rowing, but the river water starts flooding his boat, making it difficult for him to go any further. He discovers a few holes in the boat. He plugs them and manages to stop the flow of water into his boat. But this is not enough since the boat still has lots of water. With the help of a little pail, he gets rid of the accumulated water and finally crosses the river. In the same manner, a soul desirous of freedom from worldly sufferings and cycles of birth and rebirth, purifies itself and attains liberation (MOKSHA).

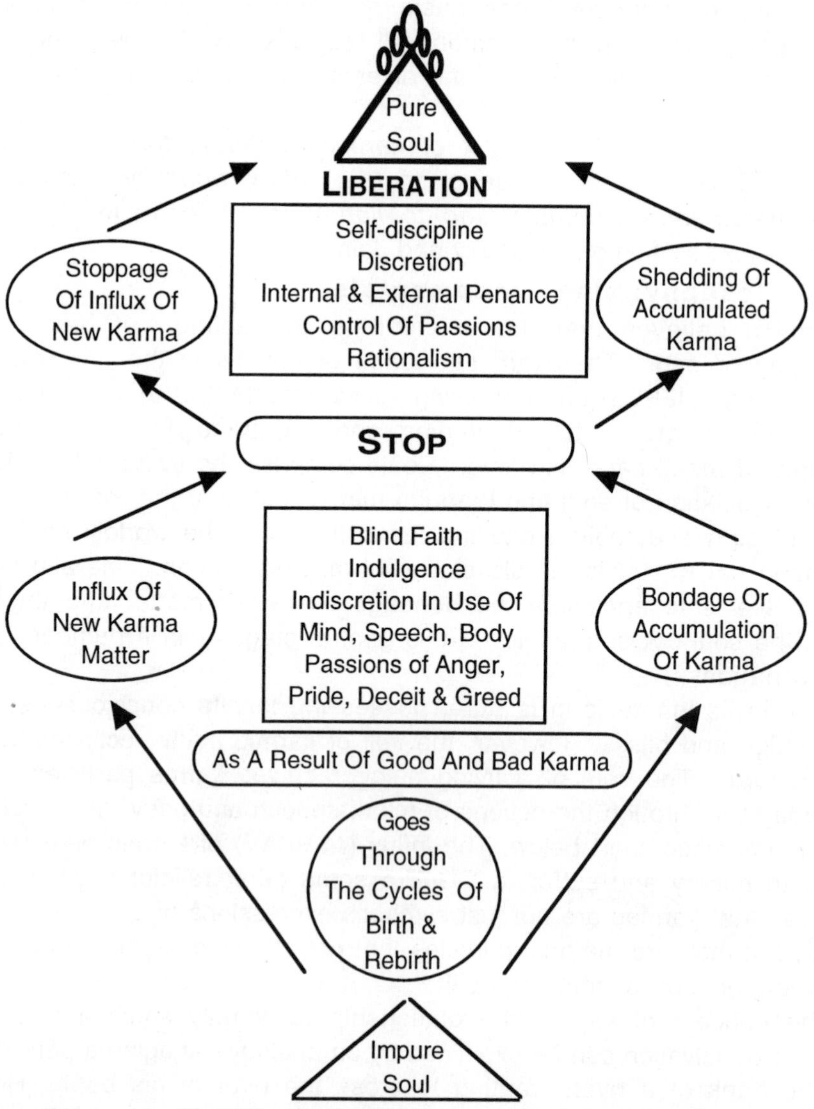


Schematic Chart Depicting Bondage of Karma and Liberation

Human life (the boat in the example) is the instrument to attain liberation. The holes in the boat are blind faith, wrong knowledge and undesirable conduct. The layers of karma accumulated in this manner (like the water flooding the boat) constitute bondage (BANDH). The process of sealing the holes, that is, preventing the influx of new karma is called SAMVAR. Getting rid of the collected water in the boat is analogous to the shedding of accumulated karma particles (NIRJARA), which ultimately leads to salvation (MOKSHA).

The processes of worldly existence and liberation of a soul involve the nine fundamentals:

1. JEEV - living
2. AJEEV - non-living
3. AASHRAV - influx
4. BANDH - bondage
5. SAMVAR - stoppage
6. NIRJARA - shedding
7. MOKSHA - salvation
8. PUNYA - good karma
9. PAAP - bad karma

These fundamentals are instrumental in the journey of the soul from the impure state to the state of perfect bliss. This theory logically explains the causes of birth and death, pain and pleasure, and defines our ultimate goal.

### The Practice Of Jainism

The two fundamentals, stoppage (SAMVAR) and shedding (NIRJARA) of karma, form the basis for Jain ethics. The need for this twofold action (stoppage of new karma and shedding of accumulated karma) provides the basis for Jain religious practices, such as equanimity (SAAMAAYIK), introspection (PRATIKRAMAN) and penance (TAPAH). The Jain code of conduct is very subtle and aims at self-restraint. Right (rational) perception (SAMYAK DARSHAN) and right knowledge (SAMYAK JNNAN) must precede Jain religious practices that constitute right conduct (SAMYAK CHARITRA). These are the means to achieve salvation.

Jain thinkers have divided society into four groups: monks (SADHUS), nuns (SADHVIS), laymen (SHRAAVAKS) and laywomen (SHRAAVIKAS). Monks and nuns practice right conduct by complete renunciation of worldly affairs and householders practice right conduct partially while carrying out their family and social responsibilities. The code of conduct is the same for all, the difference is only of degree. The aim of both groups is to lead a virtuous life by practicing the five vows: nonviolence, truth, non-stealing, celibacy and non-possessiveness, and by performing internal and external penance. The emphasis is on discipline, prudence and self-control, which lead to the stoppage of the accumulation of new karma and the shedding of old karma.

**Some Unique Features**

The Jain religion centers around the individual. It emphasizes the supremacy of soul. Jainism says that each individual is capable of attaining salvation - the pristine state of soul. Jainism believes that the universe is eternal, so there is no need for God or a creator or protector or destroyer of the universe. Hence the Jain devotee does not depend on God or on any divine power. As the universe changes on account of the interactions of the various entities that comprise it, similarly, a soul attains salvation because of its intrinsic attributes and through self-endeavor. Jains endeavor to imbibe the virtues of JIN (the Sanskrit word for victor), one who has conquered one's passions, desires and weaknesses and thus has shed all karma particles that affect one's soul. A JIN is an ideal for Jains to follow.

According to the Jain theory of karma, one enjoys and suffers the consequences of one's own karma. One does not have to depend on destiny. One can make an effort to modify the fruits of one's karma. One can shorten the duration and intensity of fruition of karmas and thus modify the course of events in one's life. Thus a person is responsible for his/her own life. In the final analysis, the liberation of one's soul is up to the individual.

Jains believe that all souls of the universe are identical. Each living being has a soul. All souls are equal and all living beings have an equal right to live. This feeling of universal "oneness" with all living beings is the basis of the Jain concept of nonviolence (AHIMSA). A similar concept of nonviolence is presented in Hindu philosophy and in other religions. However, Jainism requires us to practice this concept of nonviolence to the highest degree possible. Nonviolence is the supreme religion (अहिंसा परमो धर्मः AHIMSA PARAMO DHARMAH).

It is evident from the above discussion that Jain ethics are based on our concept of the universe and on the unique features of Jainism.

# Story Of A Worldly Soul

Retold by Shrenik Daftary[1]

Once there was a traveler named Madhubindu. He entered a village of strangers. He realized that none of the villagers would help him because they were busy with their own lives. So Madhubindu left that village and started to walk through a thick forest. In the forest, he met a wicked woman who became his traveling companion. A powerful elephant started to chase him. He started to run to get away from him, but the elephant came closer and closer to Madhubindu.

After running a considerable distance, Madhubindu came upon a huge banyan tree standing near a well. A clump of reeds grew from the wall of the well. Madhubindu was exhausted and could not run any more or climb the tree. So he jumped into the well to escape the elephant. On his way down, he grabbed a reed which was hanging into the well. The racing elephant came up to the well and tried to reach Madhubindu with his trunk. Fortunately, the elephant did not succeed.

Madhubindu found himself hanging between the tree top above and the well below. At the bottom of the well, he saw an alligator and four snakes. When he looked up, he saw two large mice, one white and one black, chewing on the reed from which he was hanging. The elephant was in rage and began to shake the tree violently. There was a beehive in the tree. The disturbance caused the bees to come out and sting Madhubindu. Occasionally, a drop of honey would fall from the beehive. Madhubindu would lick it up and forget his problems for a moment. For a split second, he would forget the snakes that were reaching out to bite him, the alligator's open mouth, the mice chewing on the reed and the elephant who was trying to uproot the tree.

At that time, a kindly couple passed by the well. They were distressed to see Madhubindu's plight. The wife persuaded the husband to try to rescue Madhubindu. Madhubindu asked them to wait until he

---

1 Son of Jyotindra and Surekha Daftary.
Slightly different versions of this parable are found in various Indian religious books. The present version has been adapted from Acharya Haribhadra's SAMARAADITYAKATHA. However, the appearance of the kindly couple representing 'religion' is from other sources.

got the drop of honey that was about to fall into his mouth. So the couple waited. But Madhubindu wanted to taste one more drop and then the next drop and so on. The couple waited for some time. Finally they gave up and left.

Eventually, the reed from which Madhubindu was hanging broke and he met the inevitable.

This story depicts the plight of a worldly being. Madhubindu represents a worldly soul. The wicked lady represents old age. The elephant is symbolic of death, which everyone has to face. The four snakes in the well represent the four passions of anger, pride, deceit and greed. The alligator represents rebirth. The reed being cut by the white and black mice represents the life-span of a living being which is continuously reduced by the bright and dark fortnights of the lunar month. The bees represent the problems we face daily, while the drops of honey represent momentary sensual pleasures. The magnanimous couple who offered to rescue Madhubindu represent religion, the entity that helps us to achieve real happiness and peace of mind.

* * * * * * *

One who is indifferent to beautiful things remains free from sorrow. He is not affected by worldly life, just as the lotus leaf is unspoiled by the water of a muddy pond.

- UTTARAADHYAYAN SUTRA

* * * * * * *

# Religion

by Shri Genda Lal Singhai[1]

Religion is grandmother,
timeworn, old, ageless,
frail figure, entangled hair;
tells stories, entertains;
also tells good from bad.
People just listen;
she continues to tell.
Can the experience of one epoch
be passed on to the next?
One does listen
but does not act.
One sits at the shore
but does not fill the pot.
One does count the waves,
but does not swim and cross the river;
does not fill the foundation of castles in air.
Who is at fault? . . . History is silent.

When the gap is bridged
between precept and deed,
then nectar and poison
will be differentiated.

---

1 English translation of a Hindi poem published in the prestigious journal TIRTHANKAR of May 1979.

## Jainism For Young Jains

by Duli Chandra Jain

Anil: Ma, today in the school cafeteria, David, Ali and I were eating lunch. David said that his religion could bring peace in the world. Ali did not agree with David and said that his (Ali's) religion could bring peace and happiness to all.

Shalini (Anil's mother): Son, what did you say?

Anil: Ma, as you had told me, I said that our Jain religion teaches nonviolence. Further, we believe that truth is many-sided. These ideas bring peace, good health and happiness in our lives.

Shalini: Son, I am happy that you understand these teachings of the Jain religion. Nonviolence is good for us and for all living beings.

Anita (Anil's sister): Ma, what are the Sanskrit words for these Jain teachings?

Shalini: The word for nonviolence is AHIMSA and the teaching that truth has many sides is called ANEKAANTAVAAD. By following these teachings, we can live peacefully with all.

Anita: Ma, I think our religion can bring peace in the world. Am I right?

Shalini: The Jain teachings bring happiness and peace in our lives. However, David and Ali are also right in their beliefs that their religions can bring peace and happiness.

Anil: Ma, how can this be right? David and Ali follow different religions. If we believe that Jainism can bring peace in the world, how can we agree that other religions too can bring peace to mankind?

Shalini: Children, think about the Jain belief that truth is many-sided. David and Ali are right from their respective viewpoints. We are right from our viewpoint. Remember that the moral teachings of all religions are similar. No religion says that violence is good. All religions want peace and happiness for all.

Anita: If the moral teachings of all religions are similar, then what is the need for different religions?

Shalini: Anita, the moral teachings of all religions are similar, but their concepts about life and man's place in the universe differ. Some religions teach that God runs the universe and that God wants people to follow their religious teachings. Jainism and some other religions teach that God does not run the affairs of the universe. So people should take care of each other and of all things, living and non-living. That is the basis for following the moral teachings of Jainism. Thus it is obvious that the followers of different religions practice the teachings of their religions for different reasons.

Anil: May I add that although all religions teach nonviolence, the degree to which we Jains practice nonviolence is higher than that followed by others?

Shalini: You are right, Anil. We try to reduce violence as much as possible.

Anita: Ma, will you please explain why we Jains practice nonviolence? Is it because God will punish us if we hurt someone? Why do we pray to Bhagwaan Mahaveer while others pray to God? Why do people make offerings to God and perform religious services?

Shalini: Children, most religions teach that God created the world and all things in it. They also believe that God rewards people for their good deeds and punishes them for their sins. That is why they avoid sins, and praise and worship God. We Jains believe that the universe was not created. It has no beginning and no end. All changes in the world take place according to the laws of nature. We believe that God does not do anything. God does not reward or punish us for our good or bad deeds. So we do not see any need to pray just to please God or gods or goddesses. Everything in our lives occurs as a result of our own thoughts and actions. We are responsible for our own lives. Other people and things do affect our lives; they may help us or hurt us.

Anil: If we ourselves are responsible for our lives, then why do we pray and worship?

Shalini: Anil, you have a good point. We learn more about the teachings of our religion by doing prayers and worship. This entails that we should know the meanings of the prayers and worship. We also have good thoughts and feelings when we visit our temples to do prayers and worship.

Anita: Ma, don't we get things like big houses, cars and fancy clothes by giving donations to temples and to the poor? Can't we avoid bad things like accidents and diseases by prayers and worship?

Shalini: Herein lies an important difference between Jainism and other religions. Although helping others is our duty, we Jains do not believe that giving donations will make us wealthy in this life or in the next life. We believe that good and bad things are part of life. Good and bad things happen in our lives because we are born and because we live in this world. We should be careful and should try to avoid bad things. When any good or bad thing happens, we should not get excited or upset. We should face everything in life calmly. No prayer or worship can help us avoid accidents and other bad things in life.

Anil: Ma, I understand that we Jains pray and worship to learn about our lives and our place in the universe. How do the moral teachings of Jainism relate to these ideas?

Shalini: The Jain religion teaches us that we should carefully observe the things around us. We should study religion, philosophy, science and other disciplines. Prayers and worship are part of our study. We should discuss what we have observed and studied with our parents, teachers and friends. This is the way to learn about our lives and about the things around us. We should think carefully and find out what is good and what is bad for us and for other living beings. The moral teachings of Jainism are based on this process of learning and thinking.

Anita: Ma, we practice nonviolence. We do not lie or steal. We keep our bodies clean and have good thoughts. We do not accumulate money and material. These are the teachings of Jainism. Why do we follow these teachings?

Shalini: To understand this, we have to grasp the meaning of violence. Violence is of two kinds; physical violence and mental violence. Physical violence means hurting or killing the self or any other living being. Mental violence means hurting the feelings of others and making them unhappy. We should remember that when we hurt others' feelings by becoming angry and hateful, by cheating, by being greedy or by taking any other undesirable action, we also hurt ourselves. When we lie or steal or have bad thoughts, we hurt others' feelings as well as our own feelings.

When we do something wrong, we are scared of being caught. This is mental violence of self. The Jain practice of nonviolence is based on our understanding of these facts.

Anita: My friend once said that animals do not have souls like ours. So men can kill them for food. Why don't we Jains kill any animals?

Shalini: We observe that animals have feelings like us. Animals love their young ones. We read the story of a cat who saved her kittens who were trapped in a fire. Animals and insects try to run away from danger. As we wish to live so do all animals. People understand these facts so they run animal shelters and try to prevent cruelty to animals. Evidently, it is not good to kill animals for food. So we Jains are vegetarians.

Anil: Ma, my teacher once said that many small insects and other living beings are hurt or killed in farming to produce fruits, vegetable and grains. Is that not violence?

Shalini: True, some violence is done in farming, but much more violence is done in producing meat. One needs about 16 pounds of grain to produce one pound of meat. Thus in addition to the violence involved in killing the animals to obtain meat, one has to commit violence in growing grains to feed the animals. Remember, we can not avoid violence completely. We can only try to minimize violence. So we eat grains, fruits and vegetables. Further, modern research has shown that non-vegetarian food is harmful to our health. We may get sick and suffer by eating non-vegetarian food. This is a form of violence of self. Moreover, non-vegetarian food spoils quickly. Thus many more living beings are produced in meat than in vegetarian food. This is one more reason why we Jains are vegetarians.

Anita: Now I understand how the knowledge of ourselves and of other things around us enlightens us to practice nonviolence. In essence, we practice nonviolence because we do not want to hurt ourselves. Nonviolence is good for us and it is good for all.

Anil: We Jains should limit the things that we possess. We should not waste things. We should limit our needs. Is this part of our practice of nonviolence?

Shalini: It certainly is. Energy and other natural resources are used in making clothes, cars and other goods. Many large and small living beings are hurt in making various things. Water and air are used and their supply is affected. We can lessen such physical violence by limiting our needs. Moreover, greed for more and more material goods is mental violence of self.

Anita: Ma, now I see the beauty of our Jain religion. Well, why does mankind have so many religions? Wouldn't it be better to have just one religion so that there are no conflicts based on religion?

Shalini: In NIYAMASAAR, Acharya Kundkund, who lived about 2000 years ago, has written: Different people have different knowledge, understanding and levels of mental development. They have different likes and dislikes. Therefore, a variety of religions and schools of thought are needed. This is the Indian way. We should tolerate different ideologies and religions. We should not try to change or convert others. Zeal for one's own religious beliefs and efforts to make others accept one's faith involve considerable violence. So it is best for us to follow our religion by practicing its teachings. This makes our lives happy and peaceful.

* * * * * * *

णाणाजीवा णाणाकम्मं णाणाविहं हवे लद्धी ।
तम्हा वयणविवादं सगपरसमएहिं वज्जिज्जो । NS-155 ।

There are various kinds of (mundane) souls, karmic bondages are of multifarious varieties, and LABDHIs (acquisition of knowledge, etc.) are of different kinds. Therefore, one should avoid entering into (mere) verbal controversies with one's own co-religionists or those professing other faiths.

- Acharya Kundkund
in NIYAM SAAR

* * * * * * *

## Jainism: A Rational Religion

Jainism attaches considerable importance to rationalism (सम्यक्त्व). Acharya Samant Bhadra, in the following couplet from RATNAKARAND SHRAAVAKAACHAAR (RS), defines religion as consisting of rational perception, rational knowledge and rational conduct:

सद्दृष्टिज्ञानवृत्तानि, धर्मं धर्मेश्वरा विदुः ।
यदीयप्रत्यनीकानि, भवन्ति भवपद्धति । RS 3 ।
SADDRISHTIJNAAN VRITTANI, DHARMAM DHARMESHVARA VIDUH
YADEEYAPRATYANEEKAANI, BHAVANTI BHAVAPADDHATI

Scholarly thinkers define religion as
rational perception, knowledge and conduct;
irrationalism – opposite of the above,
perpetuates our worldly existence.

Describing the attributes of a beneficial religion, Acharya Samant Bhadra writes:

देशयामि समीचीनं, धर्मं कर्म-निबर्हणम् ।
संसारदुःखतः सत्वान्, यो धरत्युत्तमे सुखे । RS 2 ।
DESHAYAAMI SAMEECHEENAM, DHARMAM KARMA-NIBARHANAM
SAMSAAR DHUKKHATAH SATTVAAN, YO DHARATTYUTAME SUKHE

Pristine religion is elucidated,
the liberator from all karma;
it breaks the chains of worldly grief
and helps beings attain a genuine bliss.

This indicates that religion alleviates sufferings of worldly souls. Further, practicing religion eventually leads to eternal bliss. In this respect, Acharya Umaswati presents a novel and unique concept in PRASHAMARATI PRAKARAN:

स्वर्ग सुखानि परोक्षाण्यत्यन्त परोक्षमेव मोक्षसुखम् ।
प्रत्यक्षं प्रशम सुखं न परवशं न च व्यय प्राप्तम् । 237 ।
SWARGASUKHANI PAROKSHANYATYANT
PAROKSHAMEV MOKSHASUKHAM
PRATYAKSHAM PRASHAMASUKHAM
NA PARAVASHAM NA CHA VYAYA PRAAPTAM

Happiness of heaven is obscure – beyond our experience;
(it may not interest us; it may not concern us).
Happiness of salvation is still more obscure;
(we may have skepticism about it). However,

the peace (resulting from religion) is conspicuous;
it is acquired independently by our own experience;
we do not have to spend anything to secure it.

This implies that religion plays an important role in bringing peace and happiness in our lives. Jainism says that we can achieve this through rational perception – by having a proper attitude towards life, and by understanding and accepting the real nature of things.

In TATTVAARTH SUTRA[1] (TS), Acharya Umaswati defines rational perception as:

तत्वार्थश्रद्धानं सम्यक्दर्शनम् । TS 1-2 ।
TATTVAARTH-SHRADDHAANAM SAMYAK-DARSHANAM
तन्निसर्गादधिगमाद्वा । TS 1-3 ।
TANNISARGADADHIGAMADVA

Belief in reality, that is, substances ascertained as they are, is rational perception.

Rational perception is achieved through intuition or through acquisition of reasoned knowledge (ADHIGAM).

It should be noted that rational perception is an ancient concept in Indian culture and religion. In MANUSMRITI, it is written

सम्यक् दर्शन सम्पन्नः कर्मभिर्ननिबध्यते ।
दर्शनेन विहीनस्तु संसार प्रतिपद्यते ॥
SAMYAK DARSHAN SAMPANNAH KARMABHIRNANIBHADHYATE
DARSHANEN VIHEENASTU SAMSAAR PRATIPADHYATE

A person who has acquired rational perception
does not acquire bondage of karma,
while those who do not have a proper perception
remain engrossed in this mundane world.

Rational perception is a valuable and essential attribute of a living being. In DANSAN PAAHUD, Acharya Kundkund writes:

दंसण भट्टा भट्टा दंसणभट्टस्स णत्थि णिव्वाणं ।
सिज्झंति चरिय भट्टा दंसणभट्टा ण सिज्झंति ॥
DANSAN BHATTA BHATTA DANSANBHATTASSA NATTHI NIVVAANAM
SIJJHANTI CHARIYABHATTA DANSAN BHATTA NA SIJJHANTI

People whose perception is deluded are indeed ignoble.
Such people do not attain salvation.
People with poor conduct can reform themselves,
but there is no hope for people with deluded perception.

---

1 The word SUTRA means aphorism – a short sentence stating a general truth. Prayers and scriptures containing SUTRAs as well are called SUTRAs.

By adopting rational perception, the knowledge acquired by an individual through study, observation and experience becomes rational. Further, conduct without rational knowledge is not of much avail. UTTARAADHYAYAN SUTRA (US) says:

णादंसणिस्स णाणं णाणेण विणा ण हुंति चरणगुणा ।
अगुणिस्स णत्थि मोक्खो णत्थि अमोक्खस्स णिव्वाणं ॥ US 28-30 ॥
NAADANSANISSA NAANAM NAANEN VINA NA HUNTI CHAARANAGUNA
AGUNISSA NATTHI MOKKHO NATTHI AMOKKHASSA NIVVAANAM

Knowledge is not rational without rational perception;
no rational conduct is possible without rational knowledge;
there is no liberation without rational conduct,
and there is no NIRVANA without liberation.

It should be pointed out that reasoned knowledge, which leads to rational perception, entails logical thinking. In other words, when we give up all preconceived ideas, study the scriptures and other books, listen to discourses of learned people, involve in logical thinking, and accept what seems to be reasonable according to our own experience and observation, we attain rational perception. When we embrace rational perception, our knowledge becomes rational knowledge. The conduct based on rational perception and knowledge is rational conduct. It is obvious that indulging in any activity without properly understanding its significance and meaning is irrational.

People with deluded perception blindly accept the written and spoken word on faith, without rational thinking. They accept ideas that do not conform to their observation and experience. They may indulge in superstition. They may believe in the supernatural and in superhuman powers. On the other hand, individuals having rational perception believe in reality.

The seven aspects of reality are:

जीवाजीवास्रवबन्धसंवरनिर्जरामोक्षास्तत्वम् । TS 1-4 ।
JEEV-AJEEVA-ASRAVA-BANDH-SAMVAR-NIRJARA
MOKSHAASTATTVAM

Souls (JEEV जीव)
Inanimate entities (AJEEV अजीव)
Influx of karmic matter towards a soul (ASHRAV आस्रव)
Bondage of karmic matter to a soul (BANDH बन्ध)
Stoppage of influx of karmic matter (SAMVAR संवर)
Shedding of karmic matter (NIRJARA निर्जरा)
Liberation of soul from karmic bondage (MOKSHA मोक्ष)

Some scriptures present nine aspects of reality (fundamentals) including merit (PUNYA) and demerit (PAAP). Acharya Umaswati and some other scholars include merit and demerit in influx and bondage of karma.

नामस्थापनाद्रव्यभावतस्तन्न्यासः । TS 1-5 ।

NAAM-STHAAPANA-DRAVYA-BHAAV-TASTANNYAASAH

These aspects of reality are positioned or classified through name, representation, substance (potency) and actual (real) state.

प्रमाणनयैरधिगमः । TS 1-6 ।

PRAMAAN-NAYAYAIRADHIGAMAH

Reasoned knowledge (ADHIGAM) of the aspects of reality is acquired through experimentation (PRAMAAN) and logical thinking (NAYA). Experimentation means information and evidence obtained through the study of scriptures, observation of nature and experience.

निर्देशस्वामित्वसाधनाधिकरणस्थितिविधानतः । TS 1-7 ।

NIRDESH-SWAAMITVA-SAADHANAADHIKARAN-STHITI-VIDHAANATAH

Understanding an entity or concept entails the consideration of its description (or mention), ownership, cause, place, duration and classification.

सत्संख्याक्षेत्रस्पर्शनकालान्तरभावाल्पबहुत्वैश्च । TS 1-8 ।

SAT-SAMKHYA-KSHETRA-SPARSHAN-KAALAANTAR-BHAAVAALP-BAHUTVAISHCHA

It also entails knowing its existence, number, extent, area, time, distinguishing features, quality and comparison.

Knowledge is of five kinds:

मतिश्रुतावधिमनःपर्ययकेवलानि ज्ञानम् । TS 1-9 ।

MATI-SHRUT-AVADHI-MANAAHPARYAYA-KEVALAANI JNAANAM

Sensory cognition (MATI JNAAN मति ज्ञान) – knowledge acquired through senses

Literal knowledge (SHRUT JNAAN श्रुत ज्ञान) – knowledge derived through signs, symbols, letters and words, including association, comprehension, inference, etc.

Extraordinary knowledge (clairvoyance, AVADHI JNAAN अवधि ज्ञान) – a limited ability to perceive objects and events in distant places and/or times

Mental knowledge (telepathy, MANAHAPARYAYA JNAAN मनःपर्यय ज्ञान) – ability to communicate with others mentally

Absolute knowledge (omniscience, KEVAL JNAAN केवल ज्ञान) – knowledge of absolute truth acquired by eliminating four soul-influencing karmas, viz., perception-obscuring karma, knowledge-obscuring karma, deluding karma and obstructing karma

तत्प्रमाणे । TS 1-10 ।
TATPRAMAANE
आद्ये परोक्षम् । TS 1-11 ।
AADYE PAROKSHAM
प्रत्यक्षमन्यत् । TS 1-12 ।
PRATYAKSHAMANYAT

Knowledge is derived from two types of sources (external and internal).

The first two – sensory knowledge and literal knowledge – depend on sources external to the soul. They are acquired through senses and mind. Thus these constitute indirect knowledge.

The remaining three kinds of knowledge – extraordinary knowledge, mental knowledge and absolute knowledge – are acquired directly by the soul without operation of the senses. They arise in the soul when there is destruction-cum-subsidence or destruction of karma. Thus they constitute direct knowledge.

Arya Shayyambhava, in DASHAVAIKAALIK SUTRA (DS), describes the importance of rational knowledge as follows:

पढमं नाणं तओ दया एवं चिट्ठइ सव्व संजए ।
अन्नाणी किं काही किं वा नाहिइ छेय पावगं । DS 4-10 ।
PADHAMAM NAANAM TAO DAYA EVAM CHITTHAI SAVVA SANJAYE
ANNANI KIM KAAHI KIM VA NAAHIEI CHHEYA PAAVAGAM

A person who has complete self-control
first acquires knowledge and then has compassion.
A person without knowledge indulges in actions but
what does he know about shedding demeritorious karma (PAAP)?

Arya Shayyambhava defines rational conduct in the following words:

सव्वभूयप्पभूयस्स, सम्मं भूयाइ पासओ ।
पिहिया सव्वस्स दंतस्स, पावं कम्मं न बंधई । DS 4-9 ।
SAVVABHOOYAPPABHOOYASSA SAMMAM BHOOYAAEI PAASAO
PIHIYA SAVVASSA DANTASSA PAAVAM KAMMAM NA BANDHAEI

He who treats living beings as self and
views them with equanimity, and who has checked
the influx of karma through self-control of the activities of
mind, word and deed, does not accumulate demeritorious karma.

Acharya Umaswati sums up eloquently:

सम्यक्दर्शनज्ञानचारित्राणि मोक्षमार्गः । TS 1-1 ।
SAMYAK-DARSHAN-JNAAN-CHAARITRAANI MOKSHAMAARGAH

Rational perception, rational knowledge and rational conduct together constitute the path to salvation.

## Scriptural View Of Nonviolence

Acharya Amrit Chandra Suri, in PURUSHAARTH SIDDHYUPAAYA,[1] has presented a highly sophisticated view of nonviolence, addressing numerous questions that arise in our minds.

Violence includes untruth, stealing, impurity of body and mind, and possessiveness:

आत्मपरिणामहिंसनहेतुत्वात्सर्वमेव हिंसैतत् ।
अनृतवचनादिकेवलमुदाहृतं शिष्यबोधाय ।42 ।

AATMAPARINAAMAHINSANAHETUTTVAATSARVAMEV HIMSAITAT
ANRITAVACHANAADIKEVALAMUDAHRITAM SHISHYABODHAAYA

An individual violates the pristine attributes of his/her soul by indulging in violence, untruth, stealing, impurity of body and mind, and possessiveness. Consequently, physical and mental activities involving untruth, stealing, impurity of body and mind, and possessiveness are indeed forms of violence. They have been described separately as examples of violence, only for the purpose of explaining to the aspirants.

Definition of violence:

यत्खलु कषाययोगात्प्राणानां द्रव्यभावरूपाणाम् ।
व्यपरोपणस्य करणं सुनिश्चिता भवति सा हिंसा ।43 ।

YATKHALU KASHAAYAYOGAATPRAANAANAAM DRAVYABHAAVAROOPAANAAM
VYAPAROPANASYA KARANAM SUNISHCHITA BHAVATI SA HIMSA

Violence is defined as the obstruction of the gross (DRAVYA, physical) and abstract (BHAAV, mental) life processes (PRAAN) of self and of other living beings through the activities of body, speech and mind, which originate from passions.

Definition of nonviolence:

अप्रादुर्भावः खलु रागादीनां भवत्यहिंसेति ।
तेषामेवोत्पत्तिर्हिंसेति जिनागमस्य संक्षेपः ।44 ।

---

1 English adaptation based on Sacred Books of the Jainas - Volume IV: PURUSHAARTHA SIDDHYUPAAYA, English exposition by Ajit Prasad Jain, originally published in 1933.
Most scholars believe that Acharya Amrit Chandra Suri lived in the tenth century A.D.

APRAADURBHAAVAH KHALU RAAGAADEENAAM BHAVATYAHIMSETI
TESHAAMEVOTPATTIRHIMSETI JINAAGAMASYA SAMKSHEPAH

The absence of thoughts and feelings such as attachment (RAAG), aversion (DWESH), delusion (MOHA), anger, ego, intrigue, fear, sorrow and negligence is certainly mental (BHAAV) nonviolence. The presence of such thoughts and feelings constitutes mental violence. This is the essence of the Jain scriptures.

Obstruction of life processes and nonviolence:

युक्ताचरणस्य सतो रागाद्यावेशमन्तरेणापि ।
नहि भवति जातु हिंसा प्राणव्यपरोपणादेव ।45 ।

YUKTAACHARANSYA SATO RAAGAADYAAVESHAMANTARENAAPI
NAHI BHAVATI JAATU HIMSA PRAANVYAPAROPANAADEV

Violence can not be defined simply as the obstruction of life processes. Such a definition is inadequate and incomplete. A conscientious individual whose conduct is proper and who has no improper thoughts and feelings such as attachment and aversion, does not commit any violence even when obstruction of life processes is effected.

Obstruction of life processes and violence:

व्युत्थानावस्थायां रागादीनां वशप्रवृत्तायाम् ।
म्रियतां जीवो मा वा धावत्यग्रे ध्रुवं हिंसा ।46 ।

VYUTTHAANAAVASTHAAYAAM RAAGAADEENAAM VASHAPRAVRITTAAYAAM
MRIYATAAM JEEVO MA VA DHAAVATYAGRE DHRUVAM HIMSA

On the other hand, an individual, who may or may not cause any obstruction of life processes, but if he/she indulges in the activities of body, speech and mind negligently and has feelings of attachment and aversion, certainly commits violence.

Violence of self:

यस्मात्सकषायः सन् हन्त्यात्मा प्रथममात्मनात्मानम् ।
पश्चाज्जायेत न वा हिंसा प्राण्यन्तराणां तु ।47 ।

YASMAATSAKASHAAYAH SAN HANTYAATMA PRATHAMAMAATMANAATMAANAM
PASHCHAAJJAAYET NA VA HIMSA PRAANYANTARAANAAM TU

A person, who has passions such as anger, ego and greed, commits violence of self first. Later he/she may or may not commit mental and physical violence towards other living beings.

Two situations for committing violence towards other living beings:

हिंसायामविरमणं हिंसा परिणमनमपि भवति हिंसा ।
तस्मात्प्रमत्तयोगे प्राणव्यपरोपणं नित्यम् ।48 ।

HIMSAAYAAMAVIRAMANAM HIMSA PARINAMANAMAPI BHAVATI HIMSA
TASMAATPRAMATTA YOGE PRAANAVYAPAROPANAM NITYAM

An individual commits violence through lack of abstinence and through willful activity. In both types of violence, obstruction of life processes of living beings invariably occurs through physical and mental activities involving negligence.

Violence and materialism:

सूक्ष्मापि न खलु हिंसा परवस्तु निबन्धना भवति पुंसः ।
हिंसायतननिवृत्तिः परिणामविशुद्धये तदपि कार्या ।49 ।

SOOKSHMAAPI NA KHALU HIMSA PARAVASTU NIBANDHANA BHAVATI PUMSAH
HIMSAAYATANANIVRITTIH PARINAAMAVISHUDDHAYE TADAPI KAARYAA

It has been indicated that having pristine thoughts and feelings (that are consonant with the attributes of a pure soul) is nonviolence. External materials cause attachment and aversion. Therefore, non-possessiveness is essential for the practice of nonviolence.

Absolute viewpoint and rational conduct:

निश्चयमबुध्यमानो यो निश्चयतस्तमेव संश्रयते ।
नाशयति करणचरणं स बहिः करणालसो बालः ।50 ।

NISHCHAYAMABUDDHYAMAANO YO NISHCHAYATASTAMEV SAMSHRAYATE
NAASHAYATI KARAN CHARANAM SA BAHIH KARANAALASO BAALAH

One may adopt the absolute viewpoint that pure thoughts and feelings constitute the true practice of nonviolence. Therefore, there is no harm in indulging in materialism and there is no need to adopt rational conduct. Such views disregard the fact that materialism and indulgence in sensual pleasures cause undesirable thoughts and feelings.

Importance of thoughts:

अविधायापि हि हिंसां हिंसाफलभाजनं भवत्येकः ।
कृत्वाप्यपरो हिंसा हिंसाफलभाजनं न स्यात् ।51 ।

AVIDHAAYAAPI HI HIMSA HIMSAAPHALABHAAJANAM BHAVATYEKAH
KRITVAAPYAPARO HIMSA HIMSAAPHALABHAAJANAM NA SYAAT

An individual who has thoughts of violence will certainly suffer the consequences of violence even though he/she may not commit the violence related to his/her thoughts. On the other hand, an individual, who is conscientious and has no thoughts of violence, but who becomes instrumental in some violence, faces no consequences of the violence.

## My Experience With Nonviolence

Narrated by Mool Chand Jain Pandya

At times, our religious establishments are victimized by miscreants. In such cases, instead of resorting to means that involve violence, we Jains should exhibit tolerance and understanding as exemplified by this incident.

This is a true story of fifteen idols of TEERTHANKARs that were stolen from a temple in Indore, India, in December 1981. We Jains regard that the idols of TEERTHANKARs remind us of the attributes of a pure soul. We worship these attributes and resolve to imbibe them in our lives. Thus each idol is sacred to us.

Incidents like the theft of idols are potentially explosive. They may lead to divisions in the community with one group pitted against another. They may lead to communal riots. The theft of idols was duly reported to the authorities. The police and other government agencies were on alert. They were investigating and trying to apprehend the miscreants. A reward was announced for anyone who could provide information leading to the recovery of the idols. At a meeting of the Jain community, the members of the temple committee accepted the responsibility for the untoward incident and resigned. However, the community asked them to continue.

I believe that the so-called law and order approach involves suspicion, hatred and the use of force. So the Jain community planned a parallel nonviolent course of action. Everyday, a group of people, men and women, young and old, assembled in the temple and observed fasts. The members of the temple committee also participated in the fasts. At other temples in Indore, people observed fasts in a similar manner. Prayers were said, religious songs were sung and public meetings were held. Representatives of Hindu, Sikh, Moslem and Christian religions provided their full cooperation and support at these meetings. The entire population of Indore, men, women and children, were anxious for the recovery of the idols. A committee representing all religions was formed to coordinate the efforts to protect all religious establishments. The Jain community gained valuable support from all people of Indore. There was peace and harmony.

Apparently, one of the three thieves, who had stolen the idols, was present at one of the public meetings. Later, a disagreement developed among the three. The following day, the individual who had attended the meeting came forward and admitted to the theft. The fifteen idols were returned unscathed, without a single scratch. It was a happy ending.

The return of the fifteen idols was no miracle. We believe that the nonviolent movement led to the change of heart in one of the thieves. This culminated in a disagreement among the thieves. This in itself was no modest achievement. In addition, there were other important accomplishments of our nonviolent approach. The religious gatherings, fasting, prayers and lectures by scholars of various religions turned the event into a remarkable celebration of human virtues. Instead of bitterness, suspicion and hatred, which usually result from such incidents, our method promoted feelings of love, cooperation and religious tolerance. Some young people, who did not appreciate the importance of religion in life and seldom visited a temple, participated in the effort, observed fasts and showed their concern for the well-being of the community.

Even in these trying times, nonviolence can result in the uplift of human spirit.

* * * * * * *

The basis of social institutions is peer pressure. In general, man refrains from undesirable activities such as violence and untruth because of a fear of infamy, and a craving for social status. Peer pressure keeps people in a kind of bondage. It involves a gross tendency related to fear and desire. Rules of society and the criminal justice system (unlike the teachings of religion) are subject to change. Society and government can not arrest undesirable behavior and prevent crime. Virtues such as nonviolence and truth emanate from independent thinking and from the gentle discerning instincts of human heart.

\- Acharya Shri Atmaramji

* * * * * * *

## LOGGASSA SUTRA (लोग्गस्स सूत्र)

(CHAUVEES SANTHAV, चउवीस संथव)

(Supreme Brilliance Of Universe)

I pray to TEERTHANKARs who enlighten the universe.
TEERTHANKARs reinstate the supreme religious order.
They are VEETARAAG, beyond attachment and aversion.
They conquer the inner enemies
like anger, pride, deceit and greed.
They have attained omniscience.

I pray to Rishabhadev, Ajitnath,
Sambhavanath, Abhinandan, Sumatinath,
Padmaprabh, Supaarshvanath, Chandraprabh.

I pray to Pushpadant (Suvidhinath),
Sheetalnath, Shreyaansnath, Vaasupoojya,
Vimalnath, Anantnath, Dharmnath, Shantinath.

I pray to Kunthunath, Aranath, Mallinath,
Munisuvrat, Naminath, Neminath,
Parshvanath and Mahaveer (Vardhamaan).

I pray to TEERTHANKARs who have broken
their cycles of birth and rebirth
by shedding all karma particles.
TEERTHANKARs have become
supreme souls (SIDDHAS).
May such beacons of religion
enlighten my way to spiritual progress.

The supreme souls serve as ideals
of rational perception, rational knowledge
and rational conduct.
Thus we all pray to the supreme souls.
We worship the supreme souls
with pure thoughts and feelings.
May we attain peace of mind
by following their teachings.

The supreme beings are more pristine
than millions of moons. They surpass
millions of suns in brightness.
TEERTHANKARS have become liberated souls;
they are more tranquil and serene
than the deepest oceans.
May I follow the path shown by them and eventually
attain the state of eternal bliss (NIRVANA).

* * * * * * *

The supreme souls are pristine, they are without any contamination (of attachment and aversion), they have absolute knowledge, they are invariable and eternal, they have attained their intrinsic state. I revere them with a resolve to attain my own intrinsic state.

-Acharya Amitgati in Yogasaar

* * * * * * *

## Practical Aspects Of Rationalism

Acharya Samant Bhadra (fifth century, A.D.), in RATNAKARAND SHRAAVAKAACHAAR, says that rationalism (SAMYAKTVA सम्यक्त्व) leads to happiness and peace in our lives. It ultimately leads to salvation. Rationalism includes rational perception, rational knowledge and rational conduct. These can be viewed from an absolute standpoint (निश्चय नय) and a practical standpoint (व्यवहार नय).

From the absolute standpoint, rational perception entails belief in reality. From a practical standpoint, rational perception consists of belief in supreme human beings (ARIHANTs), in the scriptures based on their teachings and in the monks who fully practice these teachings as described below.

### Rational Perception [SAMYAK DARSHAN]

Definition of rational perception:

श्रद्धानं परमार्थाना-माप्तागमतपोभृताम् ।
त्रिमूढापोढ-मष्टाङ्गं, सम्यक्दर्शनमस्मयम् ।4।

SHRADDHAANAM PARMAARTHAANAAM, APTAAGAM TAPOBHRITAAM
TRIMOODHAAPODHAMASHTAANGAM, SAMYAK DARSHANAMASMAYAM

Rational perception is belief in propitious
Supreme Beings, scriptures and sages true;
free from three kinds of superstition,
it is cultivated through virtues eight-fold.[1]

Qualities of propitious Supreme Being:

आप्तेनोच्छिन्नदोषेण, सर्वज्ञेनागमेशिना ।
भवितव्यं नियोगेन, नान्यथाह्याप्तता भवेत ।5।

AAPTENOCHHINNADOSHEN, SARVAJNENAAGAMESHINA
BHAVITAVYAM NIYOGENA, NAANYATHAAHYAAPTATA BHAVET

Propitious Supreme Beings are omniscient,
free from all blemishes like attachment and aversion;
they bestow knowledge for enrichment of all life.
One without these qualities is not auspicious.

Qualities of VEETARAAG:

क्षुत्पिपासाजरातङ्क-जन्मान्तकभयस्मयाः ।
न रागद्वेषमोहाश्च, यस्याप्तः सः प्रकीर्त्यते ।6।

1 These have been presented in Lesson 21.

KSHUTPIPAASAAJARAATANK, JANMAANTAKABHAYASMAYA
NA RAAGADWESHAMOHASHCHA, YASYAAPTAH SA PRAKEERTYATE

Propitious Beings do not have
hunger, thirst, old age, malady;
no birth, death, ego, fear and delusion,
no attachment and aversion, have such Beings.

Qualities of bestower of knowledge:

परमेष्ठी परंज्योति-विरागो विमलः कृती ।
सर्वज्ञोऽनादिमध्यान्तः, सार्वः शास्तोपलाल्यते । 7 ।

PARAMESHTHI PARAMJYOTI, VIRAAGO VIMALAH KRITI
SARVAJNOANAADIMADHYAANTAH, SAARVAH SHAASTOPALAALYATE

The supreme benevolent personality, knowing absolute truth,
dispassionate, accomplished and without soul-influencing karmas,
omniscient, who is neither the first, central nor last,
benefactor of all living beings is the bestower of knowledge.

A VEETARAAG preaches without attachment:

अनात्मार्थं विना रागैः, शास्ता शास्ति सतो हितम् ।
ध्वनन् शिल्पिकरस्पर्शान्मुरजः किमपेक्षते । 8 ।

ANAATMAARTHAM VINA RAAGAIH, SHAASTA SHAASTI SATO HITAM
DWANAN SHILPI KARASPARSHAANMURJAH KIMAPEKSHATE

The bestower of true knowledge is selfless and non-attached,
he is dispassionate and preaches for the benefit of all,
like a musical instrument, in the hands of a maestro,
that produces musical notes without any concernment.

Qualities of real scriptures:

आप्तोपज्ञमनुल्लङ्घ्य-मदृष्टेष्टविरोधकम् ।
तत्त्वोपदेशकृत्सार्वं, शास्त्रं कापथघट्टनम् । 9 ।

AAPTOPAJNAMANULLANGHYAMADDRISHTESHTAVIRODHAKAM
TATTVOPADESHKRITSAARVAM, SHASTRAM KAAPATHAGHATTANAM

Real scriptures, based on the teachings of the omniscient,
are consistent, and conform to experience and reason;
they contain the description of aspects of reality, beneficial to all;
such scriptures help us to reject the irrational path.

Qualities of a real sage (GURU):

विषयाशावशातीतो, निरारम्भोऽपरिग्रहः ।
ज्ञानध्यानतपोरक्तः, तपस्वी सः प्रशस्यते । 10 ।

VISHAYAASHAAVASHAATEETO, NIRAARAMBHOAPARIGRAHAH
JNAANADHYAANATAPORAKTAH, TAPASVI SA PRASHASYATE

An estimable sage has no passion for sensual pleasures,
has no indulgence or possessiveness,
is immersed in the pursuit of knowledge,
and is engrossed in meditation and penance.

## Rational Knowledge [SAMYAK JNAAN]

Definition of rational knowledge:

अन्यूनमनतिरिक्तं याथातथ्यं बिना च विपरीतात् ।
निःस्संदेहं वेद यदाहुस्तज्ज्ञानमागमिनः । 42 ।

ANNYOONAMANATIRIKTAM, YAATHAATATHYAM BINA CHA VIPAREETAAT
NISSANDEHAM VEDA, YADAAHUSTAJJNAANAMAAGAMINAH

Knowledge of reality as ascertained
(by observation and experience),
without omission, extrapolation, contradiction and doubt,
is called rational knowledge by the scholars of scriptures.

Primary expositions of scriptures [PRATHAMAANUYOGA]:

प्रथमानुयोगमर्थाख्यानं चरितं पुराणमपि पुण्यम् ।
बोधिसमाधिनिधानं बोधति बोधः समीचीनः । 43 ।

PRATHAMAANUYOGAMARTHAAKHYAANAM, CHARITAM PURAANAMAPI PUNYAM
BODHI SAMAADHI NIDHAANAM, BODHATI BODHAH SAMEECHEENAH

Primary expositions of scriptures contain rational knowledge
of the lives of ideal persons, who tread the path of progress,
describing righteousness, enterprise, contentment and salvation;
such knowledge enhances our rationalism and resolve.

Expositions of physical universe [KARANAANUYOGA]:

लोकालोकविभक्तेर्युगपरिवृत्तेश्चतुर्गतीनां च ।
आदर्शमिव तथामतिरवैति करणानुयोगं च । 44 ।

LOKAALOKAVIBHAKTERYUGAPARIVRITTESHCHATURGATEENAM CHA
ADARSHAMIV TATHAAMATIRAVAITI KARANAANUYOGAM CHA

The subjects of expositions of physical universe are
physical space and the space beyond it,
cycles of time and the four states of worldly existence;
these are described distinctly as reflections in a mirror.

Expositions of ethical code [CHARANAANUYOGA]:

गृहमेध्यनगाराणां चारित्रोत्पत्ति वृद्धि रक्षाङ्गम् ।
चरणानुयोग समयं सम्यक् ज्ञानं विजानाति । 45 ।

GRIHAMEDHYANAGAARAANAAM, CHAARITROTPATTI VRIDDHI RAKSHAANGAM
CHARANAANUYOGA SAMAYAM, SAMYAK JNAANAM VIJAANAATI

Expositions of the code of ethics describe
conduct for householders and for monks,
the inception, development and safeguard of such conduct;
it is an integral part of rational knowledge.

Expositions of aspects of reality [DRAVYAANUYOGA]:

जीवाजीवसुतत्वे पुण्यापुण्ये च बन्धमोक्षौ च ।
द्रव्यानुयोगदीपः श्रुतविद्यालोकमातनुते । 46 ।

JEEVAAJEEV SUTATTVE, PUNYAAPUNYE CHA BANDH MOKSHAU CHA
DRAVYAANUYOGA DEEPAH, SHRUT VIDYA LOKAMAATANUTE

Like a lamp, expositions of aspects of reality illuminate
with scriptural knowledge, living and non-living,
merit and demerit, bondage and liberation,
which are the spiritual aspects of worldly existence.

**Rational Conduct [SAMYAK CHAARITRA]**

Significance of rational conduct:

मोहतिमिरापहरणे दर्शनलाभादवाप्तसञ्ज्ञानः ।
रागद्वेषनिवृत्यै चरणं प्रतिपद्यते साधुः । 47 ।

MOHATIMIRAAPAHARANE, DARSHAN LAABHAADAVAAPTASANJNAANAH
RAAGADWESH NIVRITTYAI, CHARANAM PRATIPADYATE SAADHUH

Subsidence or partial shedding of perception-deluding karma
induces rational perception, accompanied by rational knowledge.
Consequently, by subduing conduct-deluding karma, for abating
attachment and aversion, a person pursues rational conduct.

Inception of rational conduct:

रागद्वेषनिवृत्ते हिंसादिनिवर्तना कृता भवति ।
अनपेक्षितार्थवृत्तिः कः पुरुषः सेवते नृपतीन् । 48 ।

RAAGADWESH NIVRITTE, HIMSAADI NIVARTANA KRITA BHAVATI
ANAPEKSHITAARTH VRITTIH, KAH PURUSHAH SEVATE NRIPATEEN

When attachment and aversion are subdued,
an individual abstains from violence, untruth and the like;
one loses interest in the affairs of the world;
a person without any desires seeks no favors from the rich.

What is rational conduct?

हिंसानृतचौर्येभ्यो मैथुनसेवा परिग्रहाभ्यां च ।
पापप्रणालिकाभ्यो विरतिः संज्ञस्य चारित्रम् । 49 ।

HIMSAANRIT CHAURYEBHYO, MAITHUNSEVA PARIGRAHAABHYAAM CHA
PAAPAPRANAALIKAABHYO, VIRATIH SANJNASYA CHAARITRAM

Violence, untruth, thievery, impurity of body and mind,
and possessiveness lead to influx of demeritorious karma;
a rational individual realizes this fact, and so
by avoiding these vices, adopts rational conduct.

Two kinds of rational conduct:

सकलं विकलं चरणं, तत्सकलं सर्वसङ्गविरतानाम् ।
अनगाराणां विकलं, सागाराणां ससङ्गानाम् । 50 ।

SAKALAM VIKALAM CHARANAM, TATSAKALAM SARVASANGAVIRATAANAAM
ANAGAARAANAAM VIKALAM, SAAGAARAANAAM SASANGAANAAAM

Rational conduct is of two kinds – total and partial;
total rational conduct consists of the practice of the major vows,
followed by the monks who renounce all material possessions;
the latter consists of the minor vows adopted by householders.

Three kinds of vows for householders:

गृहिणां त्रेधा तिष्ठत्यणुगुणशिक्षाव्रतात्मकं चरणम् ।
पञ्चत्रिचतुर्भेदं, त्रयं यथासंख्यमाख्यातम् । 51 ।

GRIHINAAM THREDHA TISHTHATYANUGUNA
SHIKSHAVRITAATMAKAM CHARANAM
PANCHATRICHATURBHEDAM,
TRAYAM YATHAASAMKHYAMAAKHYAATAM

The conduct of householders consists of three kinds of vows:
five partial or minor vows called ANUVRATs,[2]
three augmenting vows known as GUNAVRATs[3]
and four learning vows called SHIKSHAVRATs.[4]

Rational perception, rational knowledge and rational conduct bring contentment and happiness in our lives. They are essential for our spiritual uplift.

---

2 Lesson 13
3 Lesson 25
4 Lesson 29

Quotations From Scriptures

## Five Vows For Householders (अणुव्रत)

The five vows are nonviolence (AHIMSA), truth (SATYA), non-stealing (ACHAURYA), celibacy (purity of body and mind, BRAHMACHARYA) and non-possessiveness (APARIGRAH). These five vows are called major vows (MAHAVRAT महाव्रत) for ascetics (monks and nuns) who observe them completely. However, these are called partial or minor vows (ANUVRAT अणुव्रत) for householders who observe them partially. The following depiction of the partial vows is from Acharya Samant Bhadra's RATNAKARAND SHRAAVAKAACHAAR.

The partial vows for householders:

प्राणातिपातवितथ-व्याहारस्तेयकाममूर्छ्भ्यः ।
स्थूलेभ्यः पापेभ्यो, व्युपरमणमणुव्रतं भवति ।52 ।

PRAANAATIPAATAVITATHA-VYAAHAARASTEYAKAAMAMOORCHHEBHYAH
STHOOLEBHYAH PAAPEBHYO, VYUPARAMANAMANUVRATAM BHAVATI

Householders follow the partial vows of abstaining from undesirable activities, involving gross violence, untruth, stealing, illicit sensual pleasures and possessiveness.

The partial vow of nonviolence:

सङ्कल्पात्कृतकारित-मननाद्योगत्रयस्य चरसत्त्वान् ।
न हिनस्ति यत्तदाहुः, स्थूलवधाद्विरमणं निपुणाः ।53 ।

SANKALPAATKRITAKAARIT-MANANAADYOGATRAYASYA CHARASATVAAN
NA HINASTI YATTADAAHUH, STHOOLAVADHAADVIRAMAN NIPUNAAH

The partial vow of nonviolence entails refraining from committing or making others commit or inducing someone else to commit intentional violence of living beings of the animal kingdom, through the activities of body, speech and mind.

Transgressions of the partial vow of nonviolence:

छेदनबन्धनपीडन-मतिभारारोपणं व्यतीचाराः ।
आहारवारणाणि च, स्थूलवधाद् व्युपरतेः पञ्च ।54 ।

CHHEDANABANDHANAPEEDAN-MATIBHAARAAROPANAM VYATEECHAARAAH
AHAARAVAARANAANI CHA, STHOOLAVADHAAD VYUPARATEH PANCHAH

Transgressions of the partial vow of nonviolence are:
Mutilating a living being, restricting its movement,
inflicting pain, subjecting a beast to excessive burden
and not providing adequate food and water to animals in one's care.

The partial vow of truth:

स्थूलमलीकं न वदति, न परान् वादयति सत्यमपि विपदे ।
यत्तद्वदन्ति सन्तः, स्थूलमृषावाद-वैरमणम् ।55 ।

STHOOLAMALEEKAM NA VADATI, NA PARAAN VAADAYATI SATYAMAPI VIPADE
YATTADVADANTI SANTAH, STHOOLAMRISHAAVAAD-VAIRAMANAM

One who practices the partial vow of truth refrains from making
gross untrue statements; does not state facts to cause grief to others;
does not encourage others to indulge in such activities.
This is the precept of sagacious saints.

Transgressions of the partial vow of truth:

परिवादो रहोभ्यारव्या, पैशून्यं कूटलेखकरणं च ।
न्यासापहारितापि च, व्यतिक्रमाः पञ्च सत्यस्य ।56 ।

PARIVAADO RAHOBHYAAKHYA, PAISHOONYAM KOOTALEKHAKARANAM CHA
NYAASAAPAHAARITAAPI CHA, VYATIKRAMAAH PANCH SATYASYA

Misleading precepts, revealing confidential personal statements,
exposing other's intentions, spreading rumors and gossip,
and acquiring others' possessions by betraying their trust
are the five transgressions of the partial vow of truth.

The partial vow of non-stealing:

निहितं वा पतितं वा, सुविस्मृतं वा परस्वमविसृष्टम् ।
न हरति यन्न च दत्ते, तदकृशचौर्यादुपारमणम् ।57 ।

NIHITAM VA PATITAM VA, SUVISMRITAM VA PARASVAMAVISRISHTAM
NA HARATI YANNA CHA DATTE, TADAKRISHACHAURYAADUPAARAMANAM

The practitioner of the partial vow of non-stealing
does not usurp and does not give to someone else,
things belonging to others or lost by other persons,
or anything misplaced and forgotten by its owner.

Transgressions of the partial vow of non-stealing:

चौरप्रयोगचौरार्थी-दानविलोपसदृशसन्मिश्राः ।
हीनाधिकविनिमानं, पञ्चास्तेये व्यतीपाताः ।58 ।

CHAURAPRAYOGACHAURYAARTHA-DAANAVILOPASADRISHASANMISHRAAH
HEENAADHIKAVINIMAANAM, PANCHAASTEYE VYATEEPAATAAH

The transgressions of the partial vow of non-stealing are:
advising people to usurp others' possessions, buying stolen goods,
acquiring wealth by circumventing the laws of the land,
adulterating goods and employing counterfeit weights and measures.

The partial vow of celibacy:

न तु परदारान् गच्छति, न परान् गमयति च पापभीतेर्यत् ।
सा परदार-निवृत्तिः, स्वदारसन्तोषनामापि ।59 ।

NA TU PARADAARAAN GACHCHHATI,
NA PARAAN GAMAYATI CHA PAAPBHEETERYAT
SAA PARADAAR-NIVRITTIH, SVADAARASANTOSHANAAMAAPI

One who practices the partial vow of celibacy abstains
from going to others' spouses for sensual pleasures;
does not promote such activities done by others.
In fact, this vow inhibits physical intimacy out of wedlock.

Transgressions of the partial vow of celibacy:

अन्यविवाहाकरणा-नङ्गक्रीड़ाविटत्वविपुलतृषः ।
इत्वरिकागमनं चास्मरस्य पञ्च व्यतीचाराः ।60 ।

ANYAVIVAAHAAKARANAANANGAKREEDAVITATVAVIPULATRISHAH
ITVARIKAAGAMANAM CHAASMARASYA PANCH VYATEECHAARAAH

Arranging others' marriages, deviant sensual pleasures,
obscene language, passionate yearning for indulgence,
visiting houses of ill repute and similar establishments
are the five transgressions of the partial vow of celibacy.

The partial vow of non-possessiveness:

धनधान्यादिग्रन्थं, परिमाय ततोऽधिकेषु निस्पृहता ।
परिमितपरिग्रहः स्या-दिच्छापरिमाणनामापि ।61 ।

DHANADHAANYAADI GRANTHAM, PARIMAAYA TATOADHIKESHU NISPRIHATA
PARIMITAPARIGRAHAH SYAADICHCHHAAPARIMAANANAAMAAPI

Those who practice the partial vow of non-possessiveness
set a limit to their material possessions, movable and immovable;
they neither have attachment for materials beyond that limit
nor a burning desire for the things they do not possess.

Transgressions of the partial vow of non-possessiveness:

अतिवाहनातिसंग्रह विस्मयलोभातिभारवहनाति ।
परिमितपरिग्रहस्य च, विक्षेपा पञ्च लक्ष्यन्ते ।62 ।

ATIVAAHANAATISAMGRAH, VISMAYALOBHAATIBHAAR VAHANAATI
PARIMITAPARIGRAHASYA CHA, NIKSHEPA PANCH LAKSHYANTE

The transgressions of the partial vow of non-possessiveness are: Indulging in greed, keeping an excessive number of vehicles, carrying excessive baggage, collecting things beyond one's needs, and fascination for material wealth and comforts of others.

The five partial vows are important for contentment, happiness and peace of mind in our lives. They also create an atmosphere of understanding and trust in society.

* * * * * * *

A Scientific Basis For Relinquishing Eating At Night

In PURUSHAARTH SIDDHYUPAAYA, Acharya Amrit Chandra Suri has presented a scientific basis for relinquishing eating at night.

अर्कालोकेन विना भुञ्जानः परिहरेत् कथं हिंसाम् ।
अपि बोधितः प्रदीपे भोज्यजुषां सूक्ष्मजन्तूनाम् ।133 ।

ARKAALOKENA VINA BHUNJAANAH PRIHARET KATHAM HIMSAAM
API BODHITAH PRADEEPE, BHOJYAJUSHAAM SOOKSHAM JANTOONAAM

How is it possible to avoid (considerable) violence in consuming food after sunset? In spite of the light of lamps, a large number of minute living beings get mixed up in food.

(It is a scientific fact that fewer microorganisms are present in the atmosphere in daylight.)

* * * * * * *

# Significance Of Swastik In Jainism

by Pallavi Mehta

Jainism stresses spiritualism. It teaches that we should make an effort to uplift and purify our souls and that we should not look for material gains and comforts through religious practices. In our journey towards spiritualism, we use some symbols, mantras and prayers to take our minds away from the material world around us. SWASTIK is one such symbol.

The Sanskrit word 'SWASTI' means well-being. Thus the SWASTIK is a symbol of well-being. We use it for meditating upon soul and its place in the universe. The fours hands of SWASTIK indicate the four states of existence (GATIs) of worldly souls:

1. Human (MANUSHYA)
2. Superhuman (DEV)
3. Subhuman (TIRYANCH)
4. Hellish (NARAK)

The human state of existence is the highest of all. Only human beings can attain the status of a JIN (conqueror of inner enemies).

The four states of existence are full of suffering. Nobody is truly happy. Living beings are born; they get old and die. In order to free ourselves from the miseries of the worldly existence, we should adopt the three jewels of Jainism: rational perception (SAMYAK DARSHAN, right belief[1]), rational knowledge (SAMYAK JNAAN) and rational

1 Right belief is not identical with faith. Its authority is neither external nor autocratic. It is reasoned knowledge. One cannot doubt its testimony. So long as there is doubt, there is no right belief. But doubt

conduct (SAMYAK CHAARITRA). These are the intrinsic attributes of soul and are represented by the three circles above the SWASTIK. Adopting rational perception, rational knowledge and rational conduct comprises self-realization, which ultimately leads to liberation.

The crescent (moon in the first or last quarter) on the top of SWASTIK represents the state of existence of pure souls (SIDDHASHILA).

We use rice for SWASTIK and not any other grains for the reason that other grains grow when sown in ground but rice does not. Like rice, we do not want to be reborn. We want to end the cycle of birth and rebirth. Further, the intrinsic nature of our soul is crystal clear and pure like rice. That is why SWASTIK is drawn with rice.

In short, the features of SWASTIK epitomize our ultimate goal of salvation and the way to achieve it.

* * * * * * *

Religion in Jainism is not blind faith. Nor it is emotional worship inspired by fear or wonder. It is the intuition of the inherent purity of consciousness, will and bliss of the self.

- Dr. Nathmal Tatia

* * * * * * *

---

must not be suppressed. It must be destroyed.

- A Source Book In Indian Philosophy, edited by S. Radhakrishnan and C. A. Moore, Princeton University Press, Princeton, NJ, 1957, page 252.

## Scriptural View Of Non-Possessiveness

(APARIGRAH)

From UTTARAADHYAYAN SUTRA[1]

Root cause of misery:

ये केई सरीरे सत्ता वण्णे रूवे य सव्वसो ।
मणसा काय वक्केणं सव्वे ते दुक्ख संभवा ।6-12 ।
JE KEI SAREERE SATTA VANNE ROOVE YA SAVVASO
MANASA KAAYA-VAKKENAM SAVVE TE DUKKHA-SAMBHAVA

Those who are preoccupied in physical form, color, shape and other such attributes, with their activities of mind, body and speech, all live in misery.

Path to true happiness:

अप्पाणमेव जुज्झाहि किं ते जुज्झेण वज्झओ ।
अप्पणा चेव अप्पाणं जइत्ता सुहमेहए ।9-35 ।
APPAANAMEV JUJJHAAHI KIM TE JUJJHEN VAJJHAO
APPANA CHEV APPAANAM JAITTA SUHAMEHAE

One should fight one's inner enemies (attachment and aversion). What is the use of fighting external enemies? One who conquers one's deep-seated desires attains true happiness.

Greed knows no limits:

सव्वं जगं जइ तुहं सव्वं वा वि धणं भवे ।
सव्वं पि ते अपज्जत्तं णेव ताणाए तं तव ।14-39 ।
SAVVAM JAGAM JAI TUHAM SAVVAM VA VI DHANAM BHAVE
SAVVAM PI TE APPAJJATTAM NEV TAANAAE TAM TAVA

Even if you annex the entire universe and acquire the wealth of the whole world, it will not be sufficient to satisfy your greed. This treasure will not be able to protect you [from the miseries of the world].

Benefits of non-possessiveness:

अप्पडिबद्धयाए णं भंते! जीवे किं जणयइ?
अप्पडिबद्धयाए णं णिस्संगत्तं जणयइ ।

1 English adaptation based on UTTARAADHYAYAN SUTRA, translated into English by K. C. Lalwani, published by Prajnaanam, Calcutta, 1977, and UTTARAADHYAYAN CHAYANIKA by Dr. Kamal Chand Sogani, published by Prakrit Bharati Academy, Jaipur, 1989.

णिस्संगत्तेणं जीवे एगे एगग्गचित्ते दिया य
राओ य असज्जमाणे अप्पडिबद्धे यावि विहरइ ।29-30 ।

APPADIBADDHAYAAE NAM BHANTE! JEEVE KIM JANAYAEE?
APPADIBADDHAYAAE NAM NISSANGATTAM JANAYAEE
NISSANGATTENAM JEEVE AEGE AEGAGGACHITTE DIYA YA
RAAO YA ASAJJAMAANE APPADIBADDHE YAAVI VIHARAEE

O Venerable, what does a person gain from disinterest [in material possessions and pleasures]?

Disinterest leads to freedom from involvement. So the individual does not have to depend on external things. The individual can concentrate (on reality). Not having interest in external objects, the individual enjoys a life of independence.

Benefits of non-attachment:

वीयरागयाए णं भंते! जीवे किं जणयइ?
वीयरागयाए णं णेहाणुबंधणाणि
तण्हाणुबंधणाणि य वोच्छिंदइ मणुण्णेसु
सद्दफरिसरसरूवगंधेसु चेव विरज्जइ ।29-45 ।

VEEYARAAGAYAAE NAM BHANTE! JEEVE KIM JANAYAEE?
VEEYARAAGAYAAE NAM NEHAANUBANDHANAANI
TANHAANUBANDHANAANI YA BOCCHINDAEE MANUNNESU
SADDA-FARISA-RASA-ROOVA-GANDHESU CHEV VIRAJJAEE

O Venerable, what does a person gain by attaining the state of being beyond attachment and aversion (VEETARAAG)?

The state of VEETARAAG leads to dissolution of the bonds of attachment and possessiveness. In this state, the individual becomes detached from the sensual pleasures of sound, touch, taste, sight and smell.

Benefits of forthrightness:

अज्जवयाए णं भंते! जीवे किं जणयइ?
अज्जवयाए णं काउज्जुययं भाउज्जुययं भासुज्जुययं
अविसंवायणं जणयइ । अविसंवायणसंपण्णयाए णं
जीवे धम्मस्स आराहए भवइ ।29-48 ।

AJJAVAYAAE NAM BHANTE! JEEVE KIM JANAYAEE?
AJJAVAYAAE NAM KAAUJJUYAYAM BHAAVUJJUYAYAM
BHAASUJJUYAYAM AVISAMVAAYANAM JANAYAEE
AVISAMVAAYANASAMPANNAYAAE NAM JEEVE
DHAMMASSA ARAAHAE BHAVAEE

O Venerable, what does a person gain from forthrightness?

Forthrightness leads to unpretentious living, purity of mind and sweetness of speech. It leads to scrupulous conduct and scrupulous conduct constitutes the practice of religion (morality).

Freedom from worldly afflictions:

भावे विरत्तो मणुओ विसोगो एएण दुक्खोहपरंपरेण ।
ण लिप्पई भवमज्झे वि संतो जलेण वा पोक्खरिणी पलासं ।32-99 ।

BHAAVE VIRATTO MANUO VISOGO
AEAEN DUKKHOHAPARAMPAREN
NA LIPPAEE BHAVAMAJJHE VI SANTO
JALEN VA PUKKHARINI PALAASAM

One who is dispassionate (indifferent) about the material world has no grief. Although one is living in this world full of miseries from time immemorial, one is not affected by the afflictions of the worldly existence. One is like a lotus leaf which is not soiled by [muddy] water.

From PURUSHAARTHA SIDDHYUPAAYA
by Acharya Amrit Chandra Suri[2]

Definition of possessiveness:

या मूर्च्छा नामेयं विज्ञातव्यः परिग्रहो ह्येषः ।
मोहोदयादुदीर्णो मूर्च्छा तु ममत्व परिणामः ।111 ।

YA MOORCHHA NAAMEYAM, VIJNAATAVYAH PARIGRAHO HYESHAH
MOHODAYAADUDEERNO, MOORCHHA TU MAMATVAPARINAMAH

Affectionate regard arising from the operation of deluding karma (MOORCHHA) is possessiveness (PARIGRAH). Such possessiveness should be discarded intelligently.[3]

मूर्च्छालक्षणकरणात्सुघटा व्याप्तिः परिग्रहत्वस्य ।
सग्रन्थो मूर्च्छावान् विनाऽपि किल शेषसंगेभ्यः ।112 ।

MOORCHHA LAKSHAN KARANAT, SUGHATA VYAAPTIH PARIGRAHATVASYA
SAGRANTHO MOORCHHAAVAAN, VINAAPI KIL SHESH SANGEBHYAH

The above definition of possessiveness is comprehensively

2 English adaptation based on Sacred Books of the Jainas - Volume IV: PURUSHAARTHA SIDDHYUPAAYA, English exposition by Ajit Prasad Jain, originally published in 1933.
Most scholars believe that Acharya Amrit Chandra Suri lived in the tenth century A.D.

3 Acharya Umaswati, in TATTVARTHA SUTRA, has expressed the same concept in the aphorism MOORCHHA PARIGRAHAH:7-17:

inclusive. This means that there is no possessiveness without attachment caused by delusion. Further, if there is attachment arising from delusion, there is possessiveness. In particular, even if an individual renounces all (external) possessions but has affectionate regard caused by delusion, he/she suffers from possessiveness.

यद्येवं भवति तदा परिग्रहो न खलु कोऽपि बहिरङ्गः ।
भवति नितरां यतोऽसौ धत्ते मूर्च्छानिमित्तत्वम् ।113 ।

YADHYEVAM BHAVATI TADA, PARIGRAHO NA KHALU KOAPI BAHIRANGAH
BHAVATI NITARAAM YATOASAU, DHATTE MOORCHHA NIMITTATVAM

If affectionate regard arising from delusion is possessiveness, then how can material objects be called possessions (PARIGRAH)? The answer to the question is: Because external possessions lead to a feeling of attachment (MOORCHHA).

Internal and external possessions:

अतिसङ्क्षेपाद्विविधः स भवेदाभ्यन्तरश्च बाह्यश्च ।
प्रथमश्चतुर्दशविधो भवति द्विविधो द्वितीयस्तु ।115 ।

ATISAMKSHEPAAT DWIVIDHAH,
SA BHAVEDAABHYANTARASHCHA BAAHYASHCHA
PRATHAMASH CHATURDASHVIDHO, BHAVATI DWIVIDHO DWITEEYASTU

In brief, possessions are of two types, internal possessions and external possessions. The former are of fourteen kinds while the latter are of two kinds.

Fourteen kinds of internal possessions:

मिथ्यात्ववेदरागास्तथैव हास्यादयश्च षड्दोषाः ।
चत्वारश्च कषायाश्चतुर्दशाभ्यन्तरा ग्रन्थाः ।116 ।

MITHYAATVA VEDARAAGAAS TATHAIV HAASYAADAYASHCHA SHADDOSHAAH
CHATVAARASHCHA KASHAAYAASH CHATURDASHAABHYANTARA GRANTHAH

The following passions constitute internal possessions: Irrationalism (MITHYAATVA), three kinds of physical desires (male, female and mixed), laughter, indulgence, ennui (boredom), sorrow, fear, disgust, anger, pride, deceit and greed.

Two kinds of external possessions:

अथ निश्चित्तसचित्तौ बाह्यस्य परिग्रहस्य भेदौ द्वौ ।
नैषः कदापि सङ्गः सर्वोऽप्यतिवर्तते हिंसाम् ।117 ।

ATHA NISHCHITTA SACHITTAU, BAAHYASYA PARIGRAHASYA BHEDAU DWAU
NAISHAH KADAAPI SANGAH, SARVOAPYATIVARTATE HIMSAAM

External possessions are of two kinds: Living objects and non-living objects. All kinds of possessions [internal as well as external] involve violence.

Possessiveness is violence:

उभयपरिग्रहवर्जनमाचार्याः सूचयन्त्यहिंसेति ।
द्विविधपरिग्रहवहनं हिंसेति जिनप्रवचनज्ञाः ।118 ।

UBHAYA PARIGRAH VARJANAMAACHAARYAAH SOOCHAYANTYAHIMSETI
DWIVIDH PARIGRAH VAHANAM HIMSETI JINAPRAVACHANAJNAAH

Those who are scholars of the philosophy of JIN have enunciated that renunciation of both kinds of possessions constitutes the practice of nonviolence while keeping either kind of possession involves violence.

हिंसापर्यायत्वात्सिद्धा हिंसान्तरङ्गसङ्गेषु ।
बहिरङ्गेषु तु नियतं प्रयातु मूर्च्छैव हिंसात्वम् ।119 ।

HIMSA PARYAAYATVATSIDDHA HIMSAANTARANG SANGESHU
BAHIRANGESHU TU NIYATAM PRAYAATU MOORCHHAIVA HIMSAATVAM

Internal possessions (passions) evidently involve mental violence of self. External possessions are related to attachment caused by deluding karma and thus they constitute violence.

In summary, internal and external possessions involve physical and mental violence while non-possessiveness leads to contentment and happiness.

* * * * * * *

Even if we don't have great wealth, if we only want it and work toward it, we increase the possibilities for enmity, because we increase our chances of conflict with others who are similarly motivated. Limiting our possessions to the level of decency includes limiting our desires for more.

- Gerard A. Vanderhaar

* * * * * * *

## A Prayer To The Victors (JINS)

English adaptation of NAMOTHTHUNAM SUTRA (SHAKRASTAV)
by Shantilal Mohnot[1]

My reverence to ARIHANTs,
the destroyers of their karma,
who are BHAGWANTs[2], worthy of respect,
who were pioneers of religion,
who were TEERTHANKARs and
who reinstated the religious order.

My reverence to the supreme beings
who attained self-enlightenment,
who were supreme among humans,
who were brave like lions,
who were beyond attachment like lotuses in murky water,
who were most serene among humans like majestic elephants.

My reverence to the most illustrious in the universe,
to the supremes of the universe,
to the most beneficial in the universe,
to those who are like a brilliant light
for enlightening the universe.

The supreme beings teach us to be fearless.
They teach us to have a vision of spirituality.
They epitomize the path to liberation.
Thus they provide a shelter from worldly suffering
by leading us to self-restraint and practice of vows.

---

1 Based on PRATIKRAMAN SUTRA, edited by Muni Shree Nirvana Sagar, published by Shri Mahavira Jaina Aradhana Kendra, Koba. Slightly different versions of this prayer are found in the Jain literature.

2 The word BHAGWANT is an equivalent of Bhagwaan, the venerable.

This is the religion they cultivate.
This is the religion they preach.
The supreme beings are leaders of religion.
They are the propagators of religion.
They end the cycle of transmigration, of birth and rebirth.
They are like islands for us
who are drifting in the ocean of worldly existence.

Soul is eternal; it does not perish.
Soul has knowledge and perception.
The soul whose ignorance is gone and who has become omniscient,
the soul who is beyond attachment and aversion,
such great soul guides others to give up attachment and aversion.
Such soul crosses the ocean of transmigration
and shows others the way to accomplish the same.

The supreme beings are enlightened
and they enlighten others.
They have liberated themselves from the bondage of karma
and they show the path of salvation to others.
The omniscient ones who possess absolute perception,
who are benevolent and free from the maladies of passions,
are eternal, in an endless state of perfection.
They are beyond affliction, beyond rebirth; they are liberated.

My reverence to the souls who have conquered fear,
and have attained the state of salvation.
My reverence to JINs, the conquerors of passions.

To SIDDHAs who have attained salvation,
to ARIHANTs who are well on their way to salvation,
to all souls who are on the path to salvation,
my reverence with body, speech and mind.

## Passions: A Scriptural View

Passions are instrumental in our accumulation of karma. They cause untold miseries in life. They have adverse effects on our physical and mental being. Jain scriptures provide a detailed account of passions and their influence on our lives. The following selections are from DASHVAIKAALIK SUTRA (DS दशवैकालिक सूत्र); SUTRAKRITAANG Book 1 (SK I सूत्रकृताङ्ग प्रथम); and, UTTARAADHYAYAN SUTRA (US उत्तराध्ययन सूत्र).

कोहं माणं च मायं च लोभं च पाववड्ढणं ।
वमे चत्तारि दोसे उ इच्छंतो हियमप्पणो । DS 8- 36 ।
Anger (KRODH), pride (MAAN), intrigue (MAYA)
and greed (LOBH) augment demerit.
He who is desirous of his own well-being
should completely give up these four passions.

कोहो पीइं पणासेइ माणो विणयनासणो ।
माया मित्ताणि नासेइ लोहो सव्व विणासणो । DS 8-37 ।
Anger spoils good relations,
pride destroys humility,
intrigue is detrimental to friendship,
while greed destroys everything.

उवसमेण हणे कोहं माणं मद्दवया जिणे ।
मायं चज्जवभावेण लोभं संतोसओ जिणे । DS 8-38 ।
One should suppress anger with tranquility.
Pride should be replaced by humility.
Intrigue should be avoided through simplicity.
One should overcome greed through contentment.

कोहो य माणो य अणिग्गहीया, माया य लोभो य पवड्ढमाणा ।
चत्वारि ए ए कसिणा कसाया, सिंचंति मूलाइं पुणब्भवस्स । DS 8-39 ।
If anger and pride are not controlled, and,
if intrigue and greed are allowed to increase,
then these four evil passions serve to water
the roots of the tree of transmigration.

[The karma particles are attracted towards a worldly soul through the combined activities of body, speech and mind. These karma particles become attached to the worldly soul through the passions of anger, pride, intrigue and greed. Thus passions are the root cause of birth and rebirth.]

पूयणट्ठी जसोकामी माणसम्माणकामए ।
बहुं पसवइ पावं मायासल्लं च कुव्वई । DS 5-2-35 ।
A monk who is covetous of worship,
desirous of status, respect, name and fame,
acquires much undesirable karma; and
he indulges in deceit for hiding his blemish.

जे कोहणे होइ जगट्ठभासी, विओसियं जे उ उदीरएज्जा ।
अंधे व से दंडपहं गहाय, अविओसिए घासति पावकम्मी । SK I 13-1-5 ।
A person of wrathful disposition, who presents
bitter facts dogmatically and renews forgotten arguments,
suffers consequences of passions and evil karma,
like a blind man groping his way with a stick.

जे आवि अप्पं वसुमंति मत्ता, संखाय वायं अपरिक्ख कुज्जा ।
तवेण वाहं सहिउत्ति मत्ता, अण्णं जणं पस्सति बिंबभूयं । SK I 13-1-8 ।
He who believes himself to be firmly in control,
or unbecomingly vaunts his knowledge,
or fancies himself purified by austerities,
inaptly belittles others as mere shadows.

दुक्खं हयं जस्स न होइ मोहो, मोहो हओ जस्स न होइ तण्हा ।
तण्हा हया जस्स न होइ लोहो, लोहो हओ जस्स न किंचणाइं । US 32-8 ।
Misery ceases in the absence of delusion;
delusion ceases in the absence of desire;
desire ceases in the absence of greed;
greed ceases in the absence of possessions.

कसिणं पि जो इमं लोयं, पडिपुण्णं दलेज्ज इक्कस्स ।
तेणावि से न संतुस्से, इइ दुप्पूरए इमे आया । US 8-16 ।
If the wealth of the entire world
be bestowed lavishly on a man,

even then he is not happy;
difficult it is to attain contentment.

जहा लाहो तहा लोहो लाहा लोहो पवड्ढई ।
दोमासकयं कज्जं कोडीए वि ण णिट्ठियं । US 8-17 ।
Greed increases with possessions,
greed flares up with acquisition;
a desire for two measures of gold when fulfilled,
makes even millions of measures seem inadequate.

सुवण्णरूप्पस्स उ पव्वया भवे, सिया हु केलाससमा असंखया ।
णरस्स लुब्धस्स ण तेहिं किंचि, इच्छा हु आगाससमा अणंतिया । US 9-48 ।
Countless mounds of gold and silver,
as gigantic as Mount Kailash,
fail to satisfy a greedy individual;
desires are infinite, as vast as the sky.

पुढवी साली जवा चेव, हिरण्णं पसुभिस्सह ।
पडिपुण्णं णालमेगस्स, इइ विज्जा तवं चरे । US 9-49 ।
The entire world, full of rice and barley,
with all the stock of gold and all the cattle,
cannot satisfy the desires of a single person;
so the wise should practice austerities.

अहे वयइ कोहेण माणेणं अहमा गई ।
माया गइ पडिग्गाहो लोहाओ दुहओ भयं । US 9-54 ।
Anger causes degradation of soul;
pride leads to a low state of existence;
intrigue impedes a higher state of existence;
greed spoils both, the present and future lives.

जे पावकम्मेहि धणं मणुस्सा समाययंतो अमइं गहाय ।
पहाय ते पासपयट्टिए णरे वेराणुबद्धा णरयं उवेंति । US 4-2 ।
Men who acquire wealth with evil deeds,
by adhering to principles that are immoral,
fall into the trap (of their own passions),
with karma fetters, they go further down.

वित्तेण ताणं ण लभे पमत्ते, इमम्मि अदु वा परत्था ।
दीवप्पणट्ठेव अणंत मोहे, णेयाउअं दट्ठुमदट्ठुमेव । US 4-5 ।
Wealth helps not the careless,
to get through this world or the next;
a known road is lost when the lamp is out, so
a careless person sees not the familiar road.

सुत्तेसु आवि पडिबुद्धजीवी, ण वीससे पंडिय आसुपण्णे ।
घोरा मुहुत्ता अबलं सरीरं, भारण्डपक्खीव चरप्पमत्तो । US 4-6 ।
When others sleep, be thou awake,
trust not anyone, thou prudent and wise;
dangerous are moments, weak thy frame;
be ever alert like a BHARUNDA bird.[1]

कसायपच्चक्खाणेणं भंते ! जीवे किं जणयइ ?
कसायपच्चक्खाणेणं वीयरागभावं जणयइ ।
वीयरागभाव पडिवण्णे वि य णं जीवे समसुहदुक्खे भवइ । US 29-36 ।
O Venerable! What does the soul achieve by renouncing passions?
By renouncing passions, the soul attains a state of complete freedom, a state beyond attachment and aversion (VEETARAAG). On attaining a state free from attachment and aversion, the soul becomes dispassionate towards worldly pleasure and pain.

* * * * * * *

Just analyze the mental state of a person who works for his own gratification. For everything that he does he wants a reward. He wants a reward because there are still within him many desires controlling his very being. He has not yet conquered his lower nature. At times he becomes its slave. Now in order to liberate him from this slavish condition, the sages of the East prescribed certain guidelines. He is advised to do certain things – perform certain duties that he owes to the world, without expecting to reap any fruit from them.

\- Shri Virchand Gandhi

* * * * * * *

1 A giant bird which is ever watchful.

# 18 Bhagwaan Mahaveer And His Teachings: A Dialogue

by Duli Chandra Jain

Poonam: Today we are celebrating Mahaveer JAYANTI – the birth of Bhagwaan Mahaveer. Aneesh, do you know who Bhagwaan Mahaveer was? When was he born? Who were his parents?

Deepak: Bhagwaan Mahaveer was the twenty-fourth TEERTHANKAR of the Jains. He was born in 599 B. C. He was a contemporary of Bhagwaan Buddha, who is said to be the founder of Buddhism. His parents were King Siddharth and Queen Trishala.

Aneesh: Who are TEERTHANKARS? Are they incarnations of God?

Roopam: TEERTHANKARS are not incarnations of God. TEERTHANKARS are born as human beings. They purify their souls by getting rid of all material attachments. Thus they attain salvation. They exemplify the path to NIRVANA – the supreme spiritual state. TEERTHANKARS reinstate the religious order. Bhagwaan Mahaveer was the last TEERTHANKAR of this period in the history of Jainism.

Vineesh: Was Bhagwaan Mahaveer the founder of Jainism?

Poonam: Jainism is eternal. Like the universe, Jainism has no beginning and no end. Thus the question of any founder of Jainism does not arise.

Mohit: What are the teachings of Bhagwaan Mahaveer?

Poonam: Deepak, can you answer this question?

Deepak: The teachings of Bhagwaan Mahaveer are nonviolence (AHIMSA), truth (SATYA), non-stealing (ACHAURYA), purity of body and mind (BRAHMACHARYA) and non-possessiveness (APARIGRAH).

Vineesh: As I understand it, all religions have similar teachings. What is so unique about the teachings of Jainism?

Shalini: True, all religions have similar teachings. However, if we give it a little thought, we find that the philosophy behind the teachings of Jainism is unique. First, according to Jainism, truth, non-stealing, purity of body and mind, and non-possessiveness are part of nonviolence. Thus nonviolence is the supreme religion in Jainism. Second, Jainism teaches us to minimize mental as well as physical violence.

Deepak: We see that violence is part of life. We take a breath and innumerable living organisms are hurt. We grow wheat, corn and fruit. This involves violence. We light a fire to cook and many living beings are hurt and killed. Is such violence allowed by Jainism?

Poonam: Deepak, you ask difficult questions. Jain thinkers did realize that living in this world involves violence. Thus the question is not of allowing certain kinds of violence and prohibiting other kinds. Jainism teaches us to avoid unnecessary and intentional violence. It teaches us to minimize violence as far as possible. For example, it is not necessary to kill animals for food. So Jainism teaches vegetarianism.

Shalini: Why does Jainism lay great emphasis on nonviolence? Does God punish us for our violent actions?

Roopam: According to Jainism, physical and mental violence that is directed at others invariably leads to violence of the self. All kinds of violence is accompanied by the violence of thoughts and feelings of the person who is committing violence. In many instances, it also causes the violence of the life processes (PRAAN) of the individual. For example, when a person gets angry, his faculty of reasoning is affected and he may start to tremble. This is violence of one's own self. Jainism teaches us to minimize such violence.
As far as the question of God punishing us for our bad deeds and rewarding us for our good deeds is concerned, Jainism emphasizes freedom of the individual. It does not believe in the interference of any superhuman or supernatural power in our lives.

Shalini: I understand that there is no interference of God in our lives. Did God create the universe and does He run its affairs?

Poonam: Modern science says that the universe has no beginning and no end. Further, according to science, matter can not be created out of a void and no entity can be destroyed completely. The changes and events that take place in the universe are caused by forces of nature. These events are guided by the attributes of matter and energy. Jainism holds a similar view of the universe. So the question of creation of the universe does not arise. God, according to Jainism, is a pure soul (SIDDHA). A soul that attains the supreme spiritual state becomes God. A pure soul does not interfere with other souls and it does not interact with other entities of the universe.

Vineesh: This concept of Jainism is in agreement with modern science. Does it imply that all concepts of Jainism are scientific?

Shalini: No doubt, the basic principles of Jainism are scientific. Here the word 'scientific' means that modern science and Jainism have a common approach. Modern science and Jainism both advise us to accept only what makes sense according to our perception, observation and experience. The word 'scientific ' does not imply that all basic tenets of Jainism can be established on the basis of modern science.

Mohit: Does this mean all ideas presented in religious books or preached by a teacher are true?

Roopam: The answer to your question is at best 'maybe'. Jainism believes that only omniscients know the absolute truth. Bhagwaan Mahaveer attained omniscience. Gautam Swami,[1] Sudharm Swami and Jambu Swami, who were his disciples, were the last omniscients of the present period. After Bhagwaan Mahaveer's NIRVANA, for centuries, the scriptural knowledge given by the omniscient was transmitted from one generation to the next by word of mouth. Later, the scriptures were put into writing. In the meantime, several variations in the interpretation of scriptures had developed. Consequently, Jainism does not require us to blindly accept what is written in any book or what is preached by various teachers. We are taught to accept what is reasonable and rational.

Deepak: This discussion is getting more and more interesting. One thing comes to my mind. Jains believe that Bhagwaan Mahaveer attained omniscience. Buddhists claim that Bhagwaan Buddha attained omniscience. Some others claim that their religious personalities have preached the absolute truth. Who should we believe?

Neena: The claims of the followers of the various religions are based on their scriptures which, I believe, have come about in the same manner as the Jain scriptures. Thus the question of who to believe

---

1 Swami essentially means virtuous and venerable.

is not relevant. What to believe is important. As Shalini and Roopam said, we Jains should accept only what is rational according to our own perception, observation and experience.

Aneesh: Why do we worship Bhagwaan Mahaveer? Are we rewarded or punished by him for our deeds?

Neena: This brings us to a unique feature of Jainism. It is the concept of self-help. Neither Bhagwaan Mahaveer nor any god rewards or punishes us for our good or bad deeds. Thus Jainism is not a religion of temptation or fear. Attaining peace of mind in the present life and the supreme spiritual state in due course is up to the individual self. We worship Bhagwaan Mahaveer to remember the attributes of a pure soul. We pray to him to be reminded of our goal of spirituality. We do not pray for material favors but for spiritual advancement.

Mohit: If we pray to Bhagwaan Mahaveer for the sake of spiritual advancement, then why do we perform a variety of rituals?

Poonam: This brings us to another unique concept taught by Mahaveer Swami. At the time of Mahaveer, many rituals were performed by people with a desire to obtain material comforts in their present and future lives. Rituals were performed for curing diseases, for bringing beneficial rains, and so on and so forth. Some of these rituals even involved animal sacrifice. Priests used to accept money and materials from laymen for performing the rituals. Mahaveer said that the purpose of religion is not material comforts in the present or future lives. Religion is for attaining true happiness, which comes from peace of mind rather than from materials. This does not imply that we should not pray or worship. This only means that we should not pray or worship with a desire for material comforts. Any religious practice that is done with a desire of any kind is reduced to a meaningless ritual.

Vineesh: I have heard that karmas affect the course of our lives. What are karmas? How does one obtain karmas? Can one get rid of karmas by worship, fasting and donating money?

Roopam: Karmas are very fine particles of matter which are attached to the worldly souls. Karmas result from our emotional states such as love, anger, pride and greed. The course of our lives is determined by two factors: Karmas and pseudo-karmas (NOKARMA or NIMITTA). Our past and present karmas may determine the course of our lives. Further, our pseudo-karmas, consisting of our environment, the events taking place around us and chance, affect the course of our lives. If we have good feelings and thoughts during our religious practices, then instead of undesirable karmas, we obtain good karmas. We may even be able to get rid of some past karmas by having pure thoughts.

Mohit: Are religious practices such as prayer, worship and fasting sufficient for spiritual uplift?

Deepak: Obviously not. We should realize that our undesirable actions can not be forgiven by performing worship or charity. Further, when we indulge in a religious practice with any kind of desire, we accumulate unwelcome karmas. Bhagwaan Mahaveer said that religious practices undertaken with any kind of desires do not lead to spiritual progress. For spiritual uplift, it is essential to purify our thoughts and feelings.

Poonam: We had a good dialogue. Let us hope that we have acquired a better understanding of Bhagwaan Mahaveer's teachings today.

* * * * * * *

The belief in a supernatural agency which ordains everything has led to a certain irresponsibility on the social plane, and emotion and sentimentality have taken the place of reasoned thought and inquiry.

- Pandit Jawaharlal Nehru

* * * * * * *

# Stages of Spiritual Development

(GUNASTHAANs)

by Nirav Kumar and Sumit Kumar Vora[1]

According to Jainism, there are fourteen stages of spiritual development of a soul. They are called the GUNASTHAANs. A worldly soul goes from one spiritual stage to another as it purifies itself. Thus the path to salvation consists of fourteen steps. Each stage is higher than the previous one from a spiritual standpoint. Upon reaching the highest stage, a soul becomes a supreme soul (PARAMAATMA). It becomes a SIDDHA. Yoga – the combined activities of body, speech and mind – and the various phases of the deluding (MOHANEEYA) karma are responsible for these spiritual stages of a soul. The fourteen stages of spiritual development are the following.

1. **Deluded or irrational** (MITHYAATVA)

In the first stage, the soul is deluded or irrational on account of the operative (AUDAYIK) phase of the perception-deluding karma. Deluding karma plays a major role in the worldly existence of a soul. A soul that is under the influence of deluding karma is deeply involved in materialism and in worldly affairs. When a living being is able to suppress or subdue the deluding karma by his/her thought-activity, he/she rises up to the fourth stage which is the spiritual stage of rationalism (SAMYAKTVA).

2. **Indifferent** (SAASAADAN)

In this stage, a soul is neither rational nor irrational. A soul can fall from the fourth stage to this stage or it can fall from the fourth stage to the third and then to the second stage.

3. **Mixed or partially rational** (MISHRA)

As the name implies, in this stage, a soul is deluded in some respects and rational in other respects. This stage arises from partial shedding, partial subsidence (suppression) and partial operation of karma. In this stage, the perception-deluding karma is in the phase of partial destruction or subsidence (KSHAAYOPSHAMIK). A soul stays in

1 Sons of Dinesh C. and Saroj Vora

this stage for about forty-eight minutes (ANTARMUHURTA) and then it either rises to the fourth stage or goes down to the second stage or the first stage.

4. **Vowless rational** (AVIRAT SAMYAKTVA)

When the perception-deluding karma is in the phase of subsidence (AUPASHAMIK), shedding (KSHAAYIK) or destruction-subsidence (KSHAAYOPASHAMIK), the soul enters the vowless rational stage of spiritual development. This stage is the real entrance to the path to liberation (MOKSHA). It is the preparatory stage for a worldly being to move into the life of an ascetic. It should be pointed out that a vowless rational soul may fall to the third, second or first stage if the deluding karma which was suppressed becomes operational. On the other hand, if the deluding karma is partially destroyed, the soul may stay in the fourth stage for a considerable time.

In the fourth stage, if an individual feels disposed to and launches upon a course of self-discipline, even if partial, he or she rises to the fifth stage. Here the individual has milder passions (SANJWALAN KASHAAYA).

5. **Partial vow** (DESHAVIRAT)

In the fifth stage of spiritual development, the householders (SHRAAVAKs and SHRAAVIKAs) religiously practice the five vows of nonviolence, truth, non-stealing, partial celibacy and non-possessiveness. If these vows are practiced without rationalism, the person falls below the stage of partial vow. *In plain words, any religious practice without a clear vision of spiritualism is of not much avail.* In this stage of spiritual development, a person is devoid of intense passions of anger, pride, intrigue and greed.

Upon renouncing the worldly affairs, an individual becomes an ascetic and enters the sixth stage.

6. **Imperfect vow** (PRAMATTAVIRAT) and

7. **Perfect vow** (APRAMATTAVIRAT)

In these stages, an individual practices the five vows to the fullest extent. In these two stages as well as in the fifth stage, the conduct-deluding karma is in the phase of shedding/subsidence (suppression).

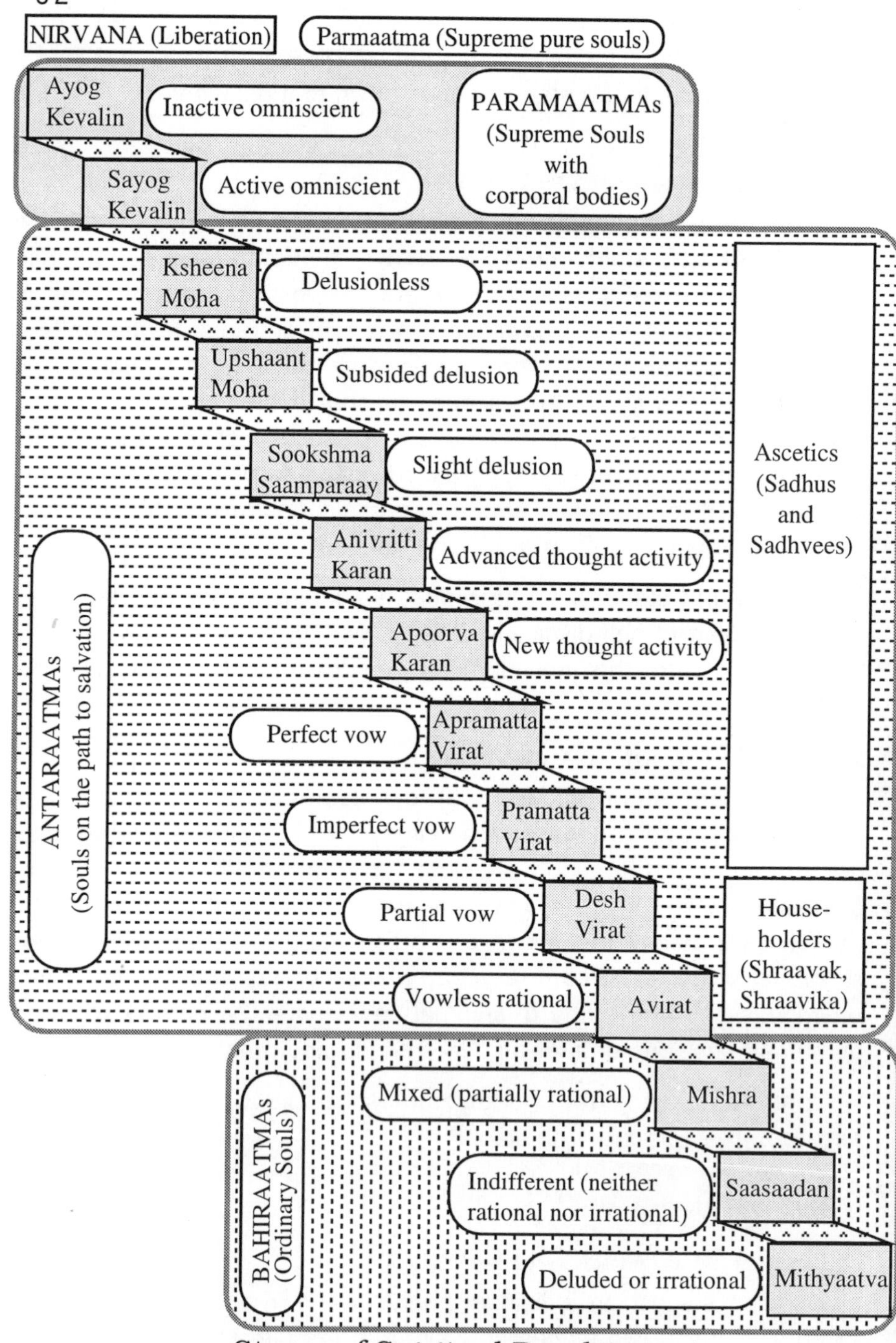


Stages of Spiritual Development

At times, the ascetic withdraws from outward activities, and fully concentrates on spiritualism. Then he or she reaches the stage of perfect vow. At other times, he or she is in the stage of imperfect vow. In these stages, the person is called MAHAAVRATI (one who practices the major vows). Passions (KASHAAYAs) and negligence (PRAMAAD) are minimal in the seventh stage. After spending ample time in the seventh stage, the ascetic begins to rise spiritually upwards to the higher stages, up to the twelfth stage, loosening the bonds of karmas and shedding them.

8. **New thought activity** (APOORVAKARAN)
9. **Advanced thought activity** (ANIVRITTIKARAN)
10. **Slight delusion** (SOOKSHMA SAAMPARAAY)
11. **Subsided delusion** (UPASHAANT MOHA)
12. **Delusion-free** (KSHEENA MOHA)

In the eighth stage, the deluding karma is in the phase of subsidence while in the ninth, tenth, eleventh and twelfth stages, the deluding karma is either in the phase of subsidence or shedding. In simple words, the ascetic gradually sheds the deluding karma associated with his or her soul.

Ultimately, in the delusion-free stage, the individual completely sheds the four soul-influencing (GHAATIYA) karmas, namely, the perception-obscuring, knowledge-obscuring, deluding and obstructing karmas. The soul attains absolute perception and knowledge, and becomes an omniscient (KEVALI). According to Jainism, only omniscients know the absolute truth. However, the absolute truth can only be experienced. According to the inexpressible aspect of relativism (SYAADVAAD), it can not be expressed in words even by an omniscient.

13. **Active omniscient** (SAYOG KEVALI)

An active omniscient is called JIN (conqueror) – he who has conquered all passions and soul-influencing karmas, and who has attained enlightenment. JINs are also called ARIHANTs – the venerable ones. All TEERTHANKARs, who preach the principles of religion for the good of all living beings, are in this stage of spiritual development.

During this stage, the omniscient has yoga (the activities of body, speech and mind) and the resulting influx of new karma particles. However, because of the absence of passions, the binding of new karma particles does not occur. Further, during this stage, although the omniscient has feeling-producing karma, he or she does not feel pleasure or pain, because, in the absence of deluding karma, feeling-producing karma has no effect.

14. **Inactive omniscient** (AYOG KEVALI)

During this stage, all activities of body, speech and mind (yoga) cease. This stage is of a very short duration. The four karmas that influence the physical being (AGHATIYA karmas), namely, the feeling-producing, life-span-determining, physique-determining and status-determining karmas are also shed by the soul. The soul becomes pure – free from all material bondage. The soul becomes liberated (SIDDHA). SIDDHAs enjoy infinite perception, knowledge and bliss for ever and ever.

Depending upon the stage of spiritual development, souls are grouped into three categories: ordinary souls (BAHIRAATMA), souls on the path to salvation (ANTARAATMA) and supreme souls (PARAMAATMA). The souls in the first three stages are BAHIRAATMAs, those in the fourth through twelfth stages are ANTARAATMAs and omniscients (KEVALIs) are PARAMAATMAs. The liberated souls (SIDDHAs) also are called PARAMAATMAs.

In conclusion, the proper course of action for us consists of coming out of the category of ordinary souls and follow the path to spiritual progress. Rationalism is the first and foremost step in this process. Prayer and worship of TEERTHANKARs, ARIHANTs and SIDDHAs, study of scriptures and various religious practices are the means to cultivate rationalism. Upon embracing rationalism, the aspirant practices the five major vows, becomes an omniscient and attains salvation. Remember, a soul becomes liberated through self-endeavor.

* * * * * * *

One who is truly devoted to one's soul, lives only for the uplift of one's soul and does not indulge in the attachment of non-soul, is a Jain. The rest are non-Jains.

- Kaka Kalelkar

* * * * * * *

## The Scrupulous Beggar: A True Story[1]

by Ayodhya Prasad Goyaliya

Once I was traveling by train. The topic of discussion was change of heart. A police chief narrated a true incident from personal experience.

He said, "Once, a beggar was walking around in my neighborhood begging for food. One of my neighbors scolded him and asked him to leave.

"I felt very sorry for him. So when he passed in front of my house, I asked him to wait and said that I would give him some food. But the beggar did not stop and continued on his way.

"I assumed that the beggar did not hear me. So I sent my servant after the beggar to give him the food.

"The beggar refused to accept the food from my servant. When my servant insisted, the beggar told him that he did not accept food and water from those who took bribes.

"My servant returned scolding the beggar and told me what the beggar had said. I was dismayed to hear the whole incident. Who had the nerve to offend a police chief? A beggar! I felt insulted. I was full of repugnance. Repeatedly, I reviled myself, my servant and the beggar.

"I asked myself why I gave sweets to a moron who, on seeing them, made such a ruckus as if someone had hurt his eyes. Why did I have to show such generosity? Granted that I made the mistake, why did the servant go after the beggar to give him food? He could have made up some excuse. He could have done something else to avoid this deplorable event. Even if the servant had gone after the beggar and that wretch had made the untoward remark, why did the servant need to tell me what the beggar said? Look at the pride of the beggar! He was begging for food and burped in public.

"I thought, 'My wife admires me only because I acquire a lot of money by accepting bribes. My sons can afford to live like princes, my friends surround me and I command the respect of my relatives

---

1 Adapted from the Hindi book, "JIN KHOJA TIN PAAINYA" by Ayodhya Prasad Goyaliya, published by Bharatiya Jnaanapith, New Delhi, 1984, page 17. English adaptation by Sunita Jain.

and of the community because of my wealth. If I do not accept bribes, then nobody will respect me because my salary is very low. It is insufficient even for my pocket expenses. If I stop taking bribes, my wife and children will not be able to live the way they want to. How will I be able to give lavish presents to my friends? How will I afford to make donations for community welfare? How will I fulfil my family obligations?'

"My heart continued to drift through ups and downs for many days. I had no peace of mind. Sometimes, the crimes of accepting bribes would appear in my mind. At times, the beggar would appear to ridicule me. Yet at other times, I would dream of the faces of my impoverished wife and children.

"Something clicked one day and I vowed not to accept any more bribes. Gradually, everybody including my relatives and friends turned away from me. I could not afford to offer gifts to my superiors at work. So I was not promoted. For a while, my heart was in agony but my willpower continued to become stronger and stronger. In spite of my well-wishers' and friends' advice and pressure, I resolved to keep my vow. Soon my mind was at peace and my monetary concerns became irrelevant.

"One year later, the same beggar came to my door. He begged for food saying that he was very hungry.

"I said to him, 'How can you accept charity from me? You know that I take bribes.'

"He smiled, called me DEVATA (a superior being) and said he knew that I had stopped taking bribes. He added that he would like to purify his body with the salt (bread) given by me and that he hoped to attain deliverance by touching the feet (by following in the footsteps) of a person as content as I.

"I reached down and touched the feet of that seer and sage."

On hearing this true story from the police chief, I (the writer) became immersed in my own thoughts. I had no desire to listen to any one else. I was gratified to know that even in this day and age of declining morality, there still were honest and contented people. My mind was filled with admiration for such individuals.

## How To Imbibe Rational Perception

Imbibing rational perception (SAMYAK DARSHAN) leads to real happiness and spiritual progress. For cultivating rational perception, Jain scriptures teach us to practice eight virtues, abstain from three kinds of misconceptions (superstitions) and refrain from eight kinds of pride. The following depiction is from Acharya Samant Bhadra's RATNAKARAND SHRAAVAKAACHAAR:

### Eight virtues for cultivating rational perception

1. Absence of suspicion [NISHSHANKIT ANGA]:

इदमेवेदृशमेव, तत्वं नान्यन्न चान्यथा ।
इत्यकम्पायसाम्भोवत्, सन्मार्गेऽसंशया रुचिः ।11 ।

IDAMEVEDRISHMEV, TATTVAM NAANYANNA CHAANYATHA
ITYAKAMPAAYASAAMBHOVAT, SANMAARGE ASANSHAYA RUCHIH

Belief in the concept of reality described by the omniscients
and in the path to spiritual uplift exemplified by them,
leads to salvation; it is the virtue of firm conviction,
like the edge of a sword that retains its sharpness.

2. Absence of desire [NISHKAANKSHIT ANGA]:

कर्मपरवशे सान्ते, दुःखैरन्तरितोदये ।
पापबीजे सुखेऽनास्था, श्रद्धानाकाङ्क्षणा स्मृता ।12 ।

KARMAPARVASHE SAANTE, DUKKHAIRANTARITODAYE
PAAPABEEJE SUKHENAASTHA, SHRADDHAANAAKAANKSHANAASMRITA

Physical pleasures and comforts result from karmas;
create dependence on external entities and are short-lived.
They eventually end in grief and cause influx of undesirable karma.
Such thoughts lead to absence of desires – this is rationalism.

3. Absence of revulsion [NIRVICHIKITSA ANGA]:

स्वभावतोऽशुचौ काये, रत्नत्रयपवित्रते ।
निर्जुगुप्सा गुणप्रीतिर्मता निर्विचिकित्सिता ।13 ।

SWABHAAVATO ASHUCHAU KAAYE, RATNATRAYA PAVITRATE
NIRJUGUPSA GUNAPREETIRMATA NIRVICHIKITSITA

Though the body is unclean by nature, it is worthy
by virtues of rational perception, knowledge and conduct.
Thus avoiding revulsion for the body, impure and ailing,
one should appreciate the beneficial aspects of human life.

4. Absence of indiscreetness [AMOODHDRISHTI ANGA]:

कापथे पथि दुःखानां, कापथस्थेऽप्यसम्मतिः ।
असम्पृक्तिरनुत्कीर्ति-रमूढा-दृष्टिरुच्यते ।14 ।

KAAPATHE PATHI DUKKHAANAAM, KAAPATHASTHE APYASAMMATIH
ASAMPRIKTIRANUTKEERTIRAMOODHA DRISHTIRUCHCHYATE

Even in the face of adversities of worldly existence, a rational person
neither accepts irrational concepts nor adopts irrational practices.
He or she does not praise or support the deeds of irrational individuals.
This is the virtue of abstaining from indiscreetness.

5. Abstinence from criticism [UPAGOOHAN ANGA]:

स्वयं शुद्धस्य मार्गस्य, बालाशक्तजनाश्रयाम् ।
वाच्यतां यत्प्रमार्जन्ति, तद्वदन्त्युपगूहनम् ।15 ।

SWAYAM SHUDDHASYA MAARGASYA, BAALAASHAKTA JANAASHRAYAAM
VAACHYATAAM YATPRAMAARJANTI, TADVADANTYUPGOOHANAM

At times, some ignorant and weak individuals indulge
in conduct inappropriate for spiritual advancement.
Those having rationalism do not defame such individuals,
and practice the virtue of abstinence from criticism.

6. Support to the beguiled [STHITIKARAN ANGA]:

दर्शनाच्चरणाद्वापि, चलतां धर्मवत्सलैः ।
प्रत्यवस्थापनं प्राज्ञैः, स्थितिकरणमुच्यते ।16 ।

DARSHANAACHCHARANAADWAAPI, CHALATAAM DHARM VATSALAIH
PRATYAVASTHAAPANAM PRAAJNAIH, STHITIKARANAMUCHYATE

A rational person helps those who are religiously disposed
but have abandoned rational perception or rational conduct.
Helping such individuals regain confidence in rationalism
constitutes the virtue of support of the religious-minded.

7. Admiration of the virtuous [VAATSALYA ANGA]:

स्वयूथ्यान्प्रति सद्भाव-सनाथापैतकैतवा ।
प्रतिपत्तिर्यथायोग्यं, वात्सल्यमभिलप्यते ।17 ।

SWAYOOTHYAAN PRATI SADBHAAV, SANAATHAAPAITAKAITAVA
PRATIPATTIRYATHAAYOGYAM, VAATSALYAMABHILAPYATE

Those possessing rationalism have feelings of goodwill for others;
they do not indulge in false, intriguing adulation;
they extend proper regard for individuals in religious pursuit;
this practice constitutes the admiration of the virtuous.

8. Advancement of the virtuous path [PRABHAAVANA ANGA]:

अज्ञानतिमिरव्याप्ति-मपाकृत्य यथायथम् ।
जिनशासनमाहात्म्य-प्रकाशः स्यात्प्रभावना ।18 ।

AJNAAN TIMIRAVYAAPTIMAPAAKRITYA YATHAAYATHAM
JINASHAASAN MAAHAATMYA, PRAKAASHAH SYAT PRABHAAVANA

Advancement of the virtuous path consists in eliminating
the darkness of irrationalism and delusion through proper conduct.
Rational practices in daily interactions with others
certainly enhance the prestige of the Jain system.

**Abstinence from three kinds of misconceptions [superstitions]**

1. Common misconceptions [LOKAMOODHHATA]:

आपगा-सागर स्नान-मुच्चयः सिकताश्मनाम् ।
गिरिपातोऽग्निपातश्च, लोकमूढं निगद्यते ।22 ।

AAPAGA SAAGAR SNAANAMUCHCHAYAH SIKATAASHMANAAM
GIRIPAATOGNIPAATASHCHA, LOKAMOODHHAM NIGADYATE

(With the intention of purifying one's soul)
taking baths in rivers and oceans,
assembling heaps of sand and rocks,
jumping off hilltops and into the fire,
constitute common misconceptions.

2. Deity-related misconceptions [DEVAMOODHHATA]:

वरोपलिप्सयाशावान्, रागद्वेषमलीमसाः ।
देवता यदुपासीत, देवतामूढमुच्यते ।23 ।

VAROPALIPSAYAASHAAVAAN, RAAGADWESHAMALIMASAH
DEVATA YADUPAASEET, DEVATAAMOODHHAMUCHYATE

With the desire of achieving material success,
with the intention of receiving blessings to that effect,
worship of gods and goddesses – symbols of attachment and aversion,
constitutes deity-related misconceptions.

3. Guru-related misconceptions [GURUMOODHHATA]:

सग्रन्थारम्भहिंसानां, संसारावर्तवर्तिनाम् ।
पाखण्डिनां पुरस्कारो, ज्ञेयं पाखण्डिमोहनम् ।24 ।

SAGRANTHAARAMBHA HIMSAANAAM, SAMSAARAAVARTAVARTINAAM
PAAKHANDINAAM PURASKAARO, JNEYAM PAAKHANDIMOHANAM

Who indulge in possessions (like ego), and in subsistence-related violence, who are involved in the pursuit of materials, perpetuating worldly existence, who, in the name of religion, propagate irrational, deluding rituals ; adoration of such monks constitutes guru-related misconceptions.

**Abstinence from eight kinds of pride**

ज्ञानं पूजां कुलं जातिं, बलमृद्धिं तपो वपुः ।
अष्टावाश्रित्य मानित्वं, स्मयमाहुर्गतस्मयाः ।25 ।

JNAANAM POOJAAM KULAM JAATIM, BALAMRIDHHIM TAPO VAPUH
ASHTAAVAASHRITYA MAANITVAM, SMAYAMAAHURGATASMAYAH

A rational individual is not proud of knowledge,
not proud of one's fame, family or community,
free from the pride of one's power and wealth,
and does not take pride in one's physique or penance.

**Conduct with rational perception**

भयाशा स्नेहलोभाच्च, कुदेवागमलिङ्गिनाम् ।
प्रणामं विनयं चैव, न कुर्युः शुद्धदृष्टयः ।30 ।

BHAYAASHA SNEHALOBHAACHCHA, KUDEVAAGAMLINGINAAM
PRANAAMAM VINAYAM CHAIVA, NA KURYUH SHUDDHHADRISHTAYAH

Individuals, who have rational perception, do not honor and respect,
on account of fear or affection or expectation or greed,
gods symbolizing attachment, gurus spreading delusions
and scriptures showing glimpses of material comforts.

If we adopt the eight virtues relating to rational perception, abstain from three kinds of misconceptions and refrain from eight kinds of pride, our lives will improve considerably.

## Significance Of Eightfold Worship

(ASHTAPRAKAARI POOJA)

by Pravin K. Shah

Jains make eight symbolic offerings during the eightfold worship. These offerings are not made to please God or gods. They are not made with the desire of any material gain. In fact, Jain worship is not performed with the purpose of curing any disease, obtaining any material comforts or achieving success in any enterprise. Jain worship is also not a celebration of material successes. Jain worship is an educational as well as a spiritual experience. It is an attempt to learn the basic teachings of the Jain religion and to understand the nature of the entities of the universe. By performing a worship, we learn about soul, karma and the path to salvation. During the worship, we should have pure thoughts and feelings, free from pride, ego, greed and the spirit of competition.

The significance of the eight kinds of offerings is as follows:[1]

1. Water (JAL) - Water is symbolic of the ocean. Worldly existence of souls is like an ocean full of desires, anxieties, disappointments and sorrow for the most part. It is perpetuated by soul's association with karma particles. We can cross this ocean and attain salvation (MOKSHA) by adopting rational perception, rational knowledge and rational conduct. With this end in view, we offer pure water before the images of TEERTHANKARs.
2. Sandalwood paste (CHANDAN) - Sandalwood paste symbolizes knowledge – knowledge of reality, of soul, of matter, of the relationship between soul and matter, of karma theory and of the means of salvation. Attaining knowledge is the first step towards liberation from the bondage of karma. To reinforce this concept, we offer sandalwood paste.
3. Flowers (PUSHP) - Flowers symbolize good conduct. Our conduct should be like a flower which provides fragrance and beauty to all without discrimination. We should have love and compassion for all living beings. Flowers are offered with such thoughts and feelings.
4. Incense (DHOOP) - Incense is a symbol of the life of an ascetic. While burning itself, incense purifies the air and spreads its

1 Different writers have associated different significance to the offerings. However, the fundamental concepts are similar.

fragrance all around. Similarly, monks and nuns devote their lives for the benefit of all people without any selfish motives of enhancing their ego or pride. The offering of incense is made with a desire to follow in the footsteps of monks and nuns.

5. Lamp (DEEP) - The flame of a lamp represents pure consciousness, that is, a soul without any bondage of karma. In Jainism, such pure souls are called SIDDHAs (liberated souls). The ultimate goal of each worldly soul is to become liberated. Offering of a lamp reminds us that by practicing the five major vows (MAHAVRATs) of total nonviolence, truth, non-stealing, celibacy and non-possessiveness, we can liberate our souls and attain salvation (NIRVANA). It reminds us of our ultimate goal of purifying our soul.
6. Rice (AKSHAT) - Rice is the kind of grain which does not grow when it is planted. It is not the seed of rice plant. Thus rice is the symbol of the state of a soul that is in its last birth. According to the Jain philosophy, a pure soul has no association with karmic matter and so it is not reborn. Offering of rice symbolizes our ultimate goal of shedding all karmas, of breaking the cycle of birth and rebirth, and of attaining the pristine state of eternal happiness.
7. Rich food (NAIVEDYA) - All worldly beings need some form of nutrition for survival. One of the afflictions of worldly souls is hunger. But supreme souls (SIDDHAs) have no bodies, no association with matter of any kind. Thus they do not suffer from hunger and they do not need any nutrition. By offering rich food, we make a determination to attain the state of supreme souls.
8. Fruit (FAL) - Fruit is the symbol of salvation (MOKSHA) – the ultimate fruit of spiritual pursuit. We can improve our lives and attain peace and happiness by reducing attachment or involvement in worldly affairs, by being indifferent towards pleasant and unpleasant things and events, by performing our duties without any expectation of reward or fear of the undesirable, and, by thinking that desirable and undesirable incidents are an inevitable part of our worldly existence. By having such an attitude, we will accumulate less karma and will be less influenced by fruition of karma, and ultimately attain salvation. The offering of fruit reminds us of our ultimate goal of NIRVANA.

All Jains, Digambar as well as Shwetambar, perform the eight-fold worship.

## 23 True Stories Of Understanding And Love

- Anonymous

We come from the land of Bhagwaan Mahaveer, Bhagwaan Krishna, Bhagwaan Buddha and Mahatma Gandhi who taught us to approach life from a different perspective. We were taught to adopt nonviolent means in dealing with others. We were also taught that nonviolent behavior creates an atmosphere of truthfulness and trust, which, in turn, influences others to treat us properly.

I used to teach in a school located in an underprivileged neighborhood. Many of the children in the school did not get proper care or support at home. Obviously, they had problems, but this was not their fault. Those children came from poor families. Many of them were being raised by single parents or relatives. They sometimes picked up some undesirable habits from their surroundings. Such children deserve our love and understanding. In view of these facts, I had to be patient with them.

Once there was a child in my class who tended to get angry and upset. I tried to reach out to him. Whenever I talked with him, he got upset. Finally, I told him that I would not speak with him until he learned to control himself. I explained to him that his problems would not be solved by getting angry or by fighting. I told him that anger not only hurts others but it also hurts the self. I asked him to talk to others calmly, without getting upset and without hurting others. I noticed that by following my advice, he began to feel better about himself. He got back his smile. At the end of the year, he thanked me and said that I had turned him into a better person.

Once a student named Dion brought a battery-operated car to the class. I thought that other students in the class would be distracted. So I asked him to leave the car in my desk which he did. Another student, George, took the car from my desk and put it in his school bag. I happened to notice that. When I went up to George, he began to shake. I told him that he was a good boy and I did not expect that kind of behavior from him. I also assured him that if he promised not to take anything without permission in the future, I would not report the matter to the principal. George said that he was sorry and made the promise. Since that day, George changed and he never picked up anything without permission. He became a conscientious student and ended up being one of the top students in the class.

A couple of years ago, two of my former students were standing in the lobby of the school. As I passed by them, a third boy who was their friend and who had not met me before, made some slighting remarks about my being an Indian and about my saree. My students did not like the remarks. They told their friend that I was their teacher and they would break his leg if he made any unpleasant remarks about me or my dress. I called my students away from their friend and told them that I did not teach them to break anybody's leg or to hurt anyone. I explained to them that violence is not the solution to any problem. Their friend had made those remarks about me because he did not know me. If he felt happy calling me names, I would not mind. Their friend overheard what I said. He felt very sorry and apologized to me.

Once I was given a difficult class of more than twenty-five children. When I took over the class, I sat down with the children and made certain rules with their suggestions. The rules were about caring and sharing, loving and trusting each other, about speaking the truth and not taking others' things without their permission. Whenever a child did not follow any of the rules, instead of punishing the child, I would talk with him or her calmly and lovingly about the rules. Things got better though not ideal. The children enjoyed learning and other people noticed the difference.

Once, at the beginning of the school year, the assistant principal gave me a note about a child who was in the habit of frequently going to the bathroom, wandering into other classes and taking things when nobody was watching. I was perplexed. I was concerned about the serious problems that child might create. But I did not know how not to trust a child. So I decided to have faith in that child and talked with him. I told him that he could go out any number of times but with my permission. I did stress the importance of learning and of making proper use of time. When the child realized that I trusted him and other children also understood this fact, things started to improve. In the matter of stealing, instead of talking with that child alone, I read the class a story explaining the importance of good moral character. I told them that good morals are more valuable than money or a piece of candy or a pen or a pencil. We also discussed the consequences of bad conduct. Though incidents happened in the school, I did not come across any improper incident in my class.

Many teachers were careful about their pocket books. They would not let their students handle them. However, I found that the more I trusted my students, the more helpful they were to me. I let my students carry my pocket book from the school entrance to the classroom. I let them open my pocket book, take out my glasses and bring them to me. Nobody stole anything from my pocket book. The children were very happy to know that I trusted them and they were always anxious to help me. At times my colleagues would tell me that my pocket book was open and they would ask me whether anything was missing from it. I do not mean to imply that nobody would ever steal anything but many thefts occur because there is mistrust and hatred. Undesirable incidents can not be prevented just by reinforcing security measures.

I noticed that children played with small toys, chewed gum, ate candy and played with coins when I was teaching. So I made a rule that everybody would place their toys, candies and coins in my desk at the beginning of the class. At the end of the school day, they would take their things from my desk. This system worked very well. No child took or claimed things belonging to another child.

At Christmas time, I put up a Christmas tree in my room just as other teachers did. I also had a small gift for each child. I told my students that it was their responsibility to see that the gifts were not misplaced. When the time of distributing the gifts came, we found that all the gifts were there. My colleagues were very surprised to learn about this.

At times, some children did get out of control, especially in the lunch room where I was not present. They threw food, ran around and had fights. In such instances, I would discuss their lunch time behavior without accusing anyone. The children who misbehaved came forward and told the truth. The faith and trust that I had in my students led to a pleasant and friendly atmosphere. I hope that when they grow up, my students will become good, honest and productive members of society.

We should remember that suspicion, hatred and misunderstanding are violence. Anger, arguments, unruly behavior and painful experiences can be avoided with love and understanding. These virtues are essential for our practice of nonviolence.

## Equanimity (SAAMAAYIK)

Equanimity is the quality of remaining calm and undisturbed. It means dwelling in one's self. It is awareness of self and of the relationship of self with the rest of the universe. It implies evenness of mind and temper. It is serenity and composure. It is essential for our practice of nonviolence. It entails removal of delusion (MOHA), attachment (RAAG) and aversion (DWESH). In fact, equanimity (SAAMAAYIK) is righteous meditation (DHARM DHYAAN). Acharya Jatasingh Nandi has presented a comprehensive definition of equanimity in the following verse:[1]

Equanimity towards all beings;
self-control and pure aspirations;
abandonment of every thought
which is tainted by desire and aversion;
that, truly, is considered SAAMAAYIK.

Equanimity is practiced by monks and nuns. It is also practiced by householders so that they can learn to gradually detach their consciousness from all external objects. Monks and nuns as well as householders renounce all undesirable activities of body, speech and mind while performing equanimity.

The practice of equanimity consists of three phases. In the first phase, which is like a prolog, the person adopts the vow of equanimity by reciting the KAREMI BHANTE SUTRA given below.[2]

I take a vow to refrain from all
undesirable physical activities,
in the entire space, for a period of
forty-eight minutes or more,
until I complete the SAAMAAYIK.

O Venerable, I consciously take this vow to perform SAAMAAYIK,
by perceptive thoughts, minding eight restraints; namely,
self-restraints (GUPTIs) of body, speech and mind,

1 The Jaina Path of Purification by Padmanabha Jaini, published by Motilal Banarsidass, Delhi, 1979, page 221

2 These SUTRAS have been adopted from SAAMAAYIK SUTRA – The Blessed Path To Emancipation, published by Khimji Nanji Sethia, Bombay.

and, conscientiousness (SAMITIs) in walking, in talking,
in accepting and placing objects and in disposal of waste.

I take the vow of refraining from all undesirable activities.
O Bhagwaan, I will worship you for the duration of SAAMAAYIK.

With the two-fold activities of doing myself or having others do,
combined with the three-fold yoga of body, speech and mind,
I will not inadvertently indulge in any undesirable activity.

O Venerable, I give up all ominous activities of speech and body.
I repent for my undesirable actions.
I express disapproval of my demerits and I resolve
to eventually free my soul from all material bondage.

The second phase of SAAMAAYIK consists of a combination of the study of scriptures, contemplation on the principles of religion and mental or vocal recitation of prayers like NAMOKAAR MANTRA.

The last phase of SAAMAAYIK is like an epilog. The following SUTRA is used for the purpose:

During the vow of SAAMAAYIK, there are
five transgressions which should be avoided;
erroneous thoughts, erroneous speech, erroneous bodily activity,
forgetfulness and improper procedure of the vow of SAAMAAYIK.
If I have committed any of these transgressions, I beg forgiveness.

During the period of SAAMAAYIK,
if my bodily activity, touch and behavior were improper,
if I did not offer complete and proper praise, respect and worship,
and, if I did not observe the teachings of the omniscient,
I beg forgiveness for these shortcomings.

There are ten faults of mind, ten faults of speech and twelve faults
of body which one can possibly commit during SAAMAAYIK.
I beg forgiveness for any faults I may have committed.

As mentioned above, there are thirty-two faults of mind, speech and body which should be avoided during SAAMAAYIK. The major faults include performing SAAMAAYIK for name and prestige or for satisfying one's ego, with a greed for wealth or for material reward. In fact, these faults should be avoided during all religious activities.

English adaptation of a few selected verses from SAAMAAYIK PAATH of Acharya Amitgati are given below. These and similar prayers are recited in the second phase of SAAMAAYIK.

O Bhagwaan, I wish to have friendly feelings for all beings,
delightful respect for the virtuous ones,
utmost compassion for the afflicted beings, and
equanimity towards those whose views are contrary to mine. /1/

O Venerable, may I remain tranquil and dispassionate
in pain or pleasure and in meeting or separation.
I wish to have composure and feelings of detachment
among friends and foes, at home and in wilderness. /3/

Passions, sensual pleasures and perverse thoughts
have resulted in my wavering from the virtuous path;
the pristine nature of my spirit has been obscured.
O Supreme, may I remedy these negative aspects. /6/

O Bhagwaan, forsaking purity of mind is misconduct;
transgressions of learning vows is indecorum;
desires for material comforts is impropriety;
indulgence in sensual pleasures constitutes immorality. /9/

I wish to emulate the supreme souls
who are free from the blemishes of worldly life,
who are absorbed in their pristine self, enjoying
the state of pure perception, knowledge and bliss. /13/

May I follow in the footsteps of great souls
who are free from material bondage and sensual desires,
beyond passions like attachment and aversion,
without worldly sufferings, immersed in infinite knowledge. /16/

Spiritualism does not entail one's own religious order
or the proximity of any virtuous personality.
Worship by others is of no avail. The need is
to renounce all worldly affairs and to realize the self. /23/

No external objects belong to me – they are of no avail;
I too do not belong to them by any measure;
I make this firm resolve regarding the external
and proceed on the path to spiritualism and liberation. /24/

On freeing the self from the whims of worldly affairs,
realizing that they cause painful material bondage,
a mendicant concentrates on the innate attributes of soul
and eventually attains the state of eternal bliss. /29/

# Augmenting Vows (गुणव्रत)

Acharya Samant Bhadra, in RATNAKARAND SHRAAVAKAACHAAR, presents the following three augmenting vows:

1. Limiting the field of activity (DIGVRAT दिग्व्रत)
2. Limiting needless activities (ANARTHADANDAVRAT अनर्थदण्डव्रत)
3. Limiting direct and indirect delectations (BHOGOPABHOGAPARIMAANAVRAT भोगोपभोगपरिमाणव्रत)

The augmenting vows of limiting one's field of activity, avoiding needless activities and limiting direct and indirect delectations provide meaningful guidelines for the daily activities of a householder. They enhance the partial vows of nonviolence, truth, non-stealing, celibacy and non-possessiveness.

The three augmenting vows:

दिग्व्रतमनर्थदण्डव्रतं च, भोगोपभोग-परिमाणं ।
अनुर्वृहणाद् गुणना-माख्यान्ति गुणव्रतान्यार्याः ।67 ।

DIGVRATAMANRTHDANDAVRATAM CHA, BHOGOPABHOGAPARIMAANAM
ANURVRIHANAAD GUNANA-MAAKHYAANTI GUNAVRATAANYAARYAAH

The augmenting vows preached by illustrious sages are:
limiting the field of activity, avoiding needless activities
and limiting the direct and indirect means of delectation.
They enhance the virtues of the partial vows for householders.

The augmenting vow of limiting the field of activity:

दिग्वलयं परिगणितं कृत्वातोऽहं बहिर्न यास्यामि ।
इति सङ्कल्पो दिग्व्रत-मामृत्यणुपापविनिवृत्त्यै ।68 ।

DIGVALAYAM PARIGANITAM KRITVAATOAHAM BAHIRNA YAASYAAMI
ITI SANKALPO DIGVRATAMAAMRITYANUPAAPAVINIVRITTYAI

The augmenting vow of limiting the field of activity entails
thoughtfully setting geographic boundaries in every direction
and making a lifetime determination of not crossing them,
for avoiding all violence outside the limit.

How to limit the field of activity?

मकराकरसरिदटवी-गिरिजनपदयोजनानि मर्या[illegible]ः ।
प्राहुर्दिशां दशानां, प्रतिसंहारे प्रसिद्धानि ।69 ।

MAKARAAKARASARIDATAVI GIRIJANAPADAYOJANAANI MARYAADAAH
PRAAHURDISHAAM DASHAANAAM PRATISAMHAARE PRASIDDHAANI

The boundaries for limiting one's field of activity
are established by using well-known oceans, rivers,
hills, mountains, districts and countries,
or by fixing distances in different directions.

Major vows outside the field of activity:

अवधेर्बहिरणुपाप-प्रतिविरते दिग्व्रतानि धारयतां ।
पञ्च महाव्रतपरिणति-मणुव्रतानि प्रपद्यन्ते ।70 ।

AWADERBAHIRANUPAAP PRATIVIRATE DIGVRATAANI DHAARAYATAAM
PANCH MAHAAVRAT PARINATIMANUVRATAANI PRAPADYANTE

By observing the augmenting vow of limiting one's field of activity,
outside the limit, a householder totally abstains from thoughts
and actions involving violence, untruth, stealing, sensual pleasures
and possessiveness, thereby observing the major vows, in a sense.

Resemblance to major vows:

प्रत्याख्यानतनुत्वान्, मन्दतराश्चरणमोहपरिणामाः ।
सत्त्वेन दुरवधारा, महाव्रताय प्रकल्प्यन्ते ।71 ।

PRATYAAKHYAAN TANUTVAAN MANDATARAASHCHARANAMOHA PARINAAMAAH
SATVEN DURAVADHAARA MAHAAVRATAAYA PRAKALPYANTE

By limiting one's field of activity, the individual subdues
the passion that obstructs complete renunciation; consequently,
the person does not experience the conduct deluding karma.
It is in this sense that the individual observes the major vows.

Definition of major vows:

पञ्चानां पापानां, हिंसादीनां मनोवचःकायैः ।
कृतकारितानुमोदै-स्त्यागस्तु महाव्रतं महताम् ।72 ।

PANCHAANAAM PAAPAANAAM HIMSADEENAAM MANOVACHAH KAAYAIH
KRITAKAARITAANUMODAISTYAAGASTU MAHAAVRATAM MAHATAAM

The five major vows entail refraining from the five vices of
violence, untruth, stealing, sensual pleasures and possessiveness,
in the activities of body, speech and mind; neither indulging in them,
nor asking others to indulge, nor supporting other's indulgence.

Transgressions of the vow of limiting the field of activity:

ऊर्ध्वाधस्तातिर्यग्-व्यतिपाताः क्षेत्रवृद्धिरवधीनाम् ।
विस्मरणं दिग्वरते-रत्याशाः पञ्च मन्यन्ते ।73 ।

OORDHWAADHASTAATIRYAG VYATIPAATAAH KSHETRA VRIDDHIRAWADHEENAAM
VISMARANAM DIGVARATERATYAASHAAH PANCH MANYANTE

Circumventing the boundaries by traveling upward or downward
or by adopting a circuitous route, altering the boundaries
and forgetting the limit constitute the transgressions of
the augmenting vow of limiting the field of activity.

The augmenting vow of limiting needless activities:

अभ्यन्तरं दिगवधे-रपार्थिकेभ्यः सपापयोगेभ्यः ।
विरमणमनर्थदण्डव्रतं, विदु-र्व्रतपरागण्यः ।74 ।

ABHYANTARAM DIGAVADHERAPAARTHIKEBHYAH SAPAAPAYOGEBHYAH
VIRAMANAMANARTHDANDAVRATAM VIDURVRATAPARAAGANYAH

The augmenting vow of avoiding needless activities
entails refraining from nonessential activities involving demerit
even within the limited field of activity. This is the teaching of
TEERTHANKARs who are eminent among aspirants.

Kinds of needless activities:

पापोपदेश हिंसादानापध्यान दुश्रुतिः पञ्च ।
प्राहुः प्रमादचर्या-मनर्थदण्डानदण्डधराः ।75 ।

PAAPOPADESH HIMSAADAANAAPADHYAAN DUSHRUTIH PANCH
PRAAHUH PRAMAADACHARYAAMANARTHADANDAANADANDADHARAAH

Those who are free from all demeritorious activities of body, speech
and mind, have described five kinds of needless activities:
promoting demeritorious activities, providing means of violence,
immoral thoughts, profane speech and reckless deeds.

Promotion of demeritorious activities:

तिर्यक्क्लेशवणिज्या-हिंसारम्भप्रलम्भनादीनाम् ।
प्रसवः कथाप्रसङ्गः स्मर्तव्यः पाप उपदेशः ।76 ।

TIRYAK KLESHA VANIJYAAHIMSAARAMBHAPRALAMBHANAADEENAAM
PRASAVAH KATHAAPRASANGAH SMARTAVYAH PAAP UPDESHAH

Promotion of demeritorious activities includes
encouraging hire and sale of animals,
setting up businesses causing grief to others
and telling stories of violence, indulgence and intrigue.

The needless activities of dealing in means of violence:

परशुकृपाणखनित्र-ज्वलनायुधशृङ्गशृङ्खलादीनाम् ।
वधहेतूनां दानं, हिंसादानं ब्रुवन्ति बुधाः ।77 ।

PARASHU KRIPAAN KHANITRA JWALANAAYUDH SHRING SHRINKHALAADEENAAM
VADHAHETOONAAM DAANAM HIMSAADAANAM BRUVANTI BUDHAAH

The needless activity of dealing in means of violence
consists of giving the instruments and implements,
such as machete, sword, firearms, poison and chains,
which can be employed to bring about violence; so say the wise.

The needless activities involving mental violence:

वधबन्धच्छेदादेर्द्वेषाद्रागाच्च परकलत्रादेः ।
आध्यानमपध्यानं, शासति जिनशासने विशदाः ।78 ।

VADHABANDHACHCHHEDAADERDWESHAADRAAGAACHCHA PARAKALATRADEH
AADHYAANAMAPADHYANAM SHAASHATI JINASHAASANE VISHADAAH

Scholars of Jainism teach that indulging in thoughts
of death, captivity and harm to others' spouses and relatives,
arising from attachment and aversion,
constitutes needless activities involving mental violence.

The needless activities involving violence of speech:

आरम्भसङ्गसाहस-मिथ्यात्वद्वेषरागमदमदनैः ।
चेतः कलुषयतां श्रुतिरवधीनां दुश्रुतिर्भवति ।79 ।

AARAMBHASANGASAAHAS MITHYATVADWESHARAAGAMADAMADANAIH
CHETAH KALUSHAYATAAM SHRUTIRAVADHEENAAM DUSHRUTIRBHAVATI

The needless activities involving violence of speech include
listening and reading episodes that defile the mind;
stories of indulgence, possessiveness, hazard,
irrationalism, aversion, attachment and lust.

The needless activities involving negligence:

क्षितिसलिलदहनपवनारम्भं विफलं वनस्पतिच्छेदम् ।
सरणं सारणमपि च, प्रमादचर्यां प्रभाषन्ते ।80 ।

KSHITISALILADAHANAPAVANAARAMBHAM VIFALAM VANASPATICHCHHEDAM
SARANAM SAARANAMAPI CHA PRAMAAD CHARYAAM PRABHAASHANTE

Nonessential activities involving digging of earth,
spilling water, lighting fires, disturbing the atmosphere,
and chopping and damaging plants and trees;
such moving and shaking constitute needless negligent acts.[1]

Transgressions of the vow of avoiding needless activities:

कन्दर्प-कौत्कुच्यं मौखर्यमतिप्रसाधनं पञ्च ।
असमीक्ष्याधिकरणं, व्यतीतयोऽनर्थदण्डकृद्विरते ।81 ।

KANDARP KAUTKUCHYAM MAUKHARYAMATIPRASAADHANAM PANCH
ASAMEEKSHYAADHIKARANAM VYATEETAYO ANARTHADANDAKRIDVIRATE

---

1 This is the message of protection of environment.

The transgressions of the vow of avoiding needless activities are:
making vulgar remarks in jest, using obscene words and gestures,
talking unnecessarily, accumulating excessive means of comfort,
and indulging in unproductive activities and enterprises.

Definition of the vow of limiting direct and indirect delectations:

अक्षार्थानां परिसंख्यानं, भोगोपभोगपरिमाणम् ।
अर्थवतामप्यवधौ, रागरतीनां तनूकृतये ।82 ।

AKSHAARTHAANAAM PARISAMKHYAANAM, BHOGOPABHOGAPARIMAANAM
ARTHAVATAAMAPYAVADHAU, RAAGARATEENAAM TANOOKRITAYE

A householder practicing the vow of non-possessiveness,
further reduces the means of material comforts,
with the intention of subduing yearning for sensual pleasures;
this is the vow of limiting direct and indirect delectations.

Direct and indirect delectations:

भुक्त्वा परिहातव्यो, भोगो भुक्त्वा पुनश्च भोक्तव्यः ।
उपभोगोऽशनवसन-प्रभृतिः पाञ्चेन्द्रियो विषयः ।83 ।

BHUKTVA PARIHAATAVYO, BHOGO BHUKTVA PUNASHCHA BHOKTAVYAH
UPBHOGO ASHAN VASAN PRABHRITIH PAANCHENDRIYO VISHAYAH

Substances such as food and clothes that gratify the senses
constitute means of direct and indirect delectations.
Means of direct delectations include food and perfume, used only once;
means of indirect ones include clothes and jewels, used time and again.

Total abstinence from non-vegetarian food, alcohol and honey:

त्रसहतिपरिहरणार्थं, क्षौद्रं पिशितं प्रसादपरिहृतये ।
मद्यं च वर्जनीयं, जिनचरणौ शरणमुपयातैः ।84 ।

TRASAHATIPARIHARANAARTHAM, KSHAUDRAM PISHITAM PRASADAPARIHRITAYE
MADYAM CHA VARJANEEYAM, JINACHARANAU SHARANAMUPYAATAIH

Those who follow the path exemplified by JIN – the victor,
avoid the violence of living beings other than plant life;
so they totally abstain from meat, alcohol and honey.
Being an intoxicant, alcohol leads to indiscretion.[2]

Abstinence from some other substances:

अल्पफलबहुविघातान्मूलकमार्द्राणि शृङ्गवेराणि ।
नवनीतनिम्बकुसुमं, कैतकमित्येवमवहेयम् ।85 ।

2 This couplet implies that non-vegetarian foods, honey and alcohol (including other intoxicants) do not fall in the domain of the vow of limiting direct and indirect means of delectation.

ALPAFALABAHUVIGHAATAANMOOLAKAMAARDRAANI SHRINGAVERAANI
NAVANEETANIMBAKUSUMAM, KAITAKAMITYEVAMAVAHEYAM

A votary does not consume vegetables that grow under the ground,
because they involve considerable violence of plant life;[3]
things like radishes, potatoes, carrots and ginger,
also some kinds of flowers and raw butter, which spoil easily.

Rationale for abstinence:

यदनिष्टं तद् व्रतयेद्यच्चानुपसेव्यमेतदपि जह्यात् ।
अभिसन्धिकृता विरतिर्विषयाद्योग्याद् व्रतं भवति ।86 ।

YADANISHTAM TAD VRATYEDYACHCHAANUPASEVYAMETADAPI JAIHYAAT
ABHISANDHIKRITA VIRATIRVISHAYAADYOGYAAD VRATAM BHAVATI

A votary abstains from objectionable substances;
he/she refrains from consuming improper substances as well.
making a resolve to give up such substances
constitutes a vow that helps in subduing sensual desires.

Lifelong abstinence and periodic abstinence:

नियमो यमश्च विहितौ, द्वेधा भोगोपभोगसंहारे ।
नियमः परिमितकालो, यावज्जीवं यमो ध्रियते ।87 ।

NIYAMO YAMASHCHA VIHITAU, DWEDHA BHOGOPABHOGASAMHAARE
NIYAMAH PARIMITAKAALO, YAAVANJEEVAM YAMO DHRIYATE

A votary can abstain from delectations in two ways;
one can give up certain delectations for the entire life
and some others for limited periods of time.
This applies to both the direct and indirect kinds.

Objects of periodic abstinence:

भोजन-वाहन-शयन-स्नान-पवित्राङ्गरागकुसुमेषु ।
ताम्बूलवसनभूषण-मन्मथसङ्गीत-गीतेषु ।88 ।

BHOJAN VAAHAN SHAYAN SNAAN PAVITRAANGARAAGAKUSUMESHU
TAAMBOOLVASANBHOOSHAN MANMATH SANGEET GEETESHU

Things to be given up for limited periods include
foods of various kinds, vehicles, sleep, lavish baths,
all cosmetics, perfumes, flowers, beetle leaves,
fancy clothes and ornaments, intimacy, songs and music.

Periods of abstinence:

अद्य दिवा रजनी वा, पक्षो मासस्तथर्तुरयनं वा ।
इति कालपरिच्छत्या, प्रत्याख्यानं भवेन्नियमः ।89 ।

3 An entire plant is destroyed in obtaining these vegetables.

ADHYA DIVA RAJANI VA, PAKSHO MAASASTATHARTURAYAM VA
ITI KAALAPARICHCHHATYA, PRATYAAKHYAANAM BHAVENNIYAMAH

When a votary refrains from direct and indirect delectations
for limited periods of time such as a few hours, a day or a night,
a week or two weeks, a month, two months or six months
the vow is known as abstinence for a limited period.

Transgressions of the vow of limiting direct and indirect delectations:

विषयविषतोऽनुपेक्षानुस्मृतिरतिलौल्यमतितृषानुभवो ।
भोगोपभोगपरिमाव्यतिक्रमाः पञ्च कथ्यन्ते ।90 ।

VISHAYAVISHATO ANUPEKSHAANUSMRITIRATILAULYAMATITRISHAANUBHAVO
BHOGOPABHOGAPARIMAAVYATIKRAMAAH PANCH KATHYANTE

The transgressions of the vow of limiting delectations are:
interest in past delectations, memories of past delectations,
intensity of desires, expectation of future sensual pleasures,
and indiscriminate absorption in present delectations.

The augmenting vows essentially teach us to conserve natural resources and thus help us in reducing violence in our lives at a personal level. In this manner, the augmenting vows send a very strong message for the preservation of our environment. Jainism teaches us to take steps to avoid problems that may arise in the future. Thus conservation of natural resources and avoiding runaway consumerism are extremely important. Modern practices, on the other hand, promote consumerism, which helps business and industry and benefits only a small segment of the world population. Mahatma Gandhi understood these facts, as is evident from the following quotation:

"To the beneficiaries of industrial growth, Gandhi's views must seem utterly out of step with reality. But . . . the industrialized world's understanding of Gandhi is severely hampered by an inability – both moral and cultural – to identify with the human tragedies and privations in which Gandhi immersed himself."[4]

---

4 Introduction to Part III of the book 'Gandhi's Significance for Today', edited by John Hick and Lamont C. Hempel, St. Martin's Press, New York, 1989, page 187.

## Significance Of Paryushan

by Seema Singhvi Jain

Paryushan, the celebration of spiritual awareness, is the most important festival of Jain religion. This annual event occurs sometime in August or September. While Shwetambar Jains observe Paryushan for eight days, Digambar Jains observe it for ten days. The latter also call it DASH LAKSHAN, the celebration of ten ultimate virtues. Paryushan is a time for self-analysis and soul searching. During Paryushan, Jains exercise self-discipline and do penance to purify their souls to the best of their individual capacities.

Paryushan has been prescribed as part of the code of conduct for monks in the last section of the sacred Jain scripture, Kalpa Sutra. During Paryushan, the monks stay in one place. This provides the householders with an opportunity to gain a deeper knowledge of Jainism from them.

It is a fact that even if we make a serious effort to live within the framework of high moral standards, we cannot avoid mistakes due to the complexities and hardships of life. During the auspicious occasion of Paryushan, we Jains review our activities of the past year in light of the teachings of Jainism and resolve to lead a spiritually cleaner life in the future. This is the purpose of celebrating Paryushan.

During Paryushan we Jains observe the vows of nonviolence, truth, non-stealing, celibacy and non-possessiveness to a greater extent than during the rest of the year. We engage in self-discipline (SANYAM) and perform penance (TAPAH) such as study of scriptures (SWAADHYAAYA), partial or complete fasting, introspection (PRATIKRAMAN) and repentance (PRAAYASHCHITTA). We observe modesty, forgiveness and renunciation. Throughout Paryushan, we Jains attend religious discourses given by scholars. We also resolve to make a greater effort towards spiritual progress in the coming year.

Many Jains do not eat after sunset because sunlight is a natural disinfectant and thus bacterial content in the atmosphere is less during the daytime. Some Jains do not eat vegetables grown underground because entire plants are destroyed in obtaining them. During Paryushan, most Jains observe these rules and do not eat green vegetables. Some Jains observe an eight-day fast (ATHAAI), drinking only boiled water. Others observe a complete fast (ANASHAN) for a day, or partial fast (EKAASHAN - eating once a day, or BE-ASAN - eating only twice a day). During these fasts, one's thoughts and feelings should be pure and free from passions such as anger, pride, intrigue and greed.

The first three days of Paryushan are devoted to the three jewels of Jainism – rational perception, rational knowledge and rational conduct. The fourth day of Paryushan is known as TAPAH DIVAS (penance day). The fifth day is SAPANA DIVAS (day of dreams). On this day, the fourteen dreams of Trishala Devi are displayed and Bhagwaan Mahaveer's birth is celebrated. The sixth day is the day of self-control (SANYAM) and the seventh day is the day of purification of soul (ATMA SHUDDHI). On the last day of Paryushan which is known as SAMVATSARI, we Jains perform collective introspection (PRATIKRAMAN).[1] This is called SAAMVATSARIK PRATIKRAMAN.

In the Digambar tradition, Paryushan is a celebration of the following ten ultimate virtues (DASH LAKSHAN):

1. Ultimate Forgiveness (UTTAM KSHAMA)
2. Ultimate Modesty (UTTAM MAARDAV)
3. Ultimate Straightforwardness (UTTAM ARJAV)
4. Ultimate Truthfulness (UTTAM SATYA)
5. Ultimate Cleanliness of thoughts and feelings (UTTAM SHAUCH)
6. Ultimate Self-control (UTTAM SANYAM)
7. Ultimate Penance (UTTAM TAPAH)
8. Ultimate Renunciation (UTTAM TYAAG)
9. Ultimate Non-attachment (UTTAM AKINCHAN)
10. Ultimate Purity of body and mind (UTTAM BRAHMCHARYA)

Each day one chapter from Acharya Umaswati's TATTVAARTH SUTRA is recited and its meaning is explained and discussed. Further, each day the importance of one of the ten ultimate virtues is elucidated.

At the end of Paryushan, we Jains, with a clear conscience, request

1 Presented in Lesson 27.

forgiveness from each other and from all living beings of the universe for our thoughts, speech and actions by which we might have hurt others' feelings. We recite the following Universal Forgiveness Prayer known as KSHAMAAPANA SUTRA:

I grant forgiveness to all living beings.
May all living beings grant me forgiveness.
My friendship is with all living beings.
My enmity is totally non-existent.

The celebration of Paryushan is espied all over the world. Jains are held in high esteem on account of their belief in nonviolence and their practice of austerities, especially during Paryushan. The great Mogul Emperor Akbar was deeply impressed by Jainism. Because of the influence of Shwetambar Jain Acharya Shri Hiravijaya Suri, he had issued a proclamation prohibiting the killing of animals during Paryushan. Paryushan brings about spiritual awareness and progress.

* * * * * * *

From SHANTIPARV of MAHABHARAT

Equanimity (समता)

आत्मनीष्टे तथानिष्टे रिपौ च समता तथा ।
इच्छाद्वेषक्षयं प्राप्य कामक्रोधक्षयं तथा ॥11॥

Equanimity entails maintaining similar feelings for a dear friend and for an arch enemy. It is attained through the conquest of desires (attachment), aversion, sensual pleasures and anger.

Renunciation (त्याग)

त्यागः स्नेहस्य यत् त्यागो विषयाणां तथैव च ।
रागद्वेषप्रहीणस्य त्यागो भवति नान्यथा ॥17॥

A genuine renunciation entails relinquishing infatuation and sensual pleasures. Renunciation is realized by relinquishing attachment and aversion – not by any other means.

* * * * * * *

## Introspection (PRATIKRAMAN)

by Falgunee Parekh[1]

Man is the most intelligent among all living beings. We have the most control over improving our lives. We are aware of the fact that one who is born will die someday. Some depart this life in peace, others do not. Some people accomplish considerable spiritual progress while others do not. What makes the difference? Traveling on the path of truth and happiness makes the difference. But, how do we achieve it? Being human, we do make some mistakes and go on the wrong path, intentionally or unintentionally. However, life is not a one-way street. We can always go back and correct our mistakes. Then we return to the right path of truth and happiness. PRATIKRAMAN (introspection) is the process of returning from the wrong path to the right path. For this, we have to engage in self-analysis, self-realization and introspection. All these constitute PRATIKRAMAN. The goal of PRATIKRAMAN is to minimize the impact of our mistakes on our lives and to make an effort so that such mistakes are not repeated.[2]

There are five types of PRATIKRAMAN:

1. DEVASI PRATIKRAMAN is performed in the evening to reflect on the transgressions of vows (wrongdoings) done during the day.
2. RAYI PRATIKRAMAN which is performed in the morning to reflect on the mistakes and transgressions of vows done at night.
3. PAKKHI PRATIKRAMAN which is done fortnightly.
4. CHOMASI PRATIKRAMAN which is done once every four months, on the day of the full moon during the KAARTIK, FAALGUN and ASHAADH months of the Indian calendar.
5. SAMVATSARI PRATIKRAMAN is done once a year at the end of PARYUSHAN, the celebration of spiritual awareness. PARYUSHAN

---

1 Daughter of Kishor and Jayshree Parekh

2 In general, people think that PRATIKRAMAN is performed to get rid of sins. However, in Jainism, the concept of sin is somewhat different from that in other religions. In Jainism, sin (PAAP) consists of bad karma particles attached to our souls. These karma particles can be transformed by having good thoughts and feelings. In this sense our religious practices such as PRATIKRAMAN are beneficial. It is the transformations and modifications of karma particles which may lead to lesser impact of our improprieties on our lives. We should remember that all kinds of thought activities, good and bad, cause the influx of karma towards our soul. - D. C. J.

and SAMVATSARI PRATIKRAMAN are the most auspicious occasions for Jains. All Jains are expected to perform SAMVATSARI PRATIKRAMAN.

PRATIKRAMAN consists of six segments:

1. Equanimity (SAAMAAYIK) is the first step of introspection. This entails being in the proper frame of mind, the state of calmness which is undisturbed by joy, sorrow, success or failure.
2. Prayer (CHAUVISANTHO or STUTI) is the worship of twenty-four TEERTHANKARs to purify our thoughts and to get rid of anger, pride, greed, etc.
3. Obeisance (VANDANA) is the offering of reverence to all those whose virtuous conduct and teachings serve as ideals for us. We revere the pure souls (SIDDHAs) because our ultimate goal is to purify our souls by removing the bondage of karma. We revere TEERTHANKARs and other supreme human beings (ARIHANTs) because they show us the path to liberation from karma. We revere the monks and teachers who are spiritually advanced. We learn modesty and give up false pride through devotion to pure souls, supreme human beings and teachers. We start on the path to spiritual progress shown by the supreme human beings, obtain scriptural knowledge and ultimately attain salvation (MOKSHA).
4. Introspection (PRATIKRAMAN) is the main segment which is basically recalling the wrongdoings and resolving not to repeat them. It also includes asking forgiveness for our wrongdoings from those who are affected by our deeds and forgiving those whose actions are offensive in our view.[3]
5. Renunciation of body (KAAYOTSARG) which implies mental detachment from our physical being and minimization of the activities of our body, speech and mind. This is for conditioning of our physical being so that we do not feel the influence of the elements.
6. Resolution (PRATYAAKHYAAN) - In this last segment, we resolve to practice the five vows of nonviolence, truth, non-stealing, purity of body and mind and non-possessiveness in our daily lives. We resolve to have pure thoughts and indulge in righteous activities.[4]

PRATIKRAMAN helps us to attain peace of mind, true happiness and spiritual progress. It puts us on the path to salvation.

---

3 We should express these ideas to our relatives, friends and colleagues when we meet them. - D. C. J.

4 TIRTHANKAR (Hindi), Volume 14, Issue 6/7, 1984.

# Delwara Jain Temples

by Sunita Jain

Delwara Jain temples are called 'hymns in marble.' These magnificent temples are famous all over the world for their unparalleled and unique marble architecture. They belong to the rich cultural heritage of Jains.

Delwara temples are located among high hills covered with palm trees on Mount Abu about 2000 ft above sea level. In ancient times, Mount Abu was called ARBUD. It is located in the Indian state of Rajasthan and can be easily reached from the cities of Udaipur, Jodhpur, Ajmer, Jaipur and Delhi. It is about 120 miles from the city of Ahmedabad. The Government of India has developed Mount Abu as a tourist attraction.

There are five Jain temples on Mount Abu: Vimal Vasahi, Luna Vasahi, Pitalhar Temple, Khartar Vasahi and Temple of Mahaveer Swami. Vimal Vasahi and Luna Vasahi are built of white marble. They are the oldest and most beautiful of the five temples. Vimal Vasahi was built in 1032 A.D. by Vimal Shah, the chief minister of Bhimadev I, Solanki ruler of Gujarat. The temple has a main inner sanctum and a number of cells around it. Inside the richly carved doorway of the sanctum is an idol of Bhagwaan Rishabhadev. Two standing marble idols of Bhagwaan Parshvanath in meditation are on either side of the main idol. The cells contain idols of TEERTHANKARs, idols of gods and goddesses, scenes depicting important events in the lives of TEERTHANKARs and legends from ancient Indian culture.

Vimal Vasahi contains beautifully carved pillars, ceilings, domes and arches. It also has a grand hall (RANG MANDAP). Its sculptured dome is supported by 12 elaborately carved marble columns connected with arches. One has to see it to fully appreciate its beauty. It is said that Vimal Vasahi was built by 1500 artisans and 1200 laborers in 15 years time at a cost of about 180 million rupees.

Prithvipal, a descendent of Vimal Shah, carried out some improvement and renovation of Vimal Vasahi in 1147-49 A.D. To commemorate the event, he built an elephant chamber (HASTISHALA) containing ten large marble elephants in front of the temple. In 1311 A.D., the Muslim ruler, Ala-Uddin Khilji, destroyed Vimal Vasahi and damaged the idols. Since then, the temple has been reconstructed and repaired twice.

Luna Vasahi is the second marble temple built in 1232 A.D., at a cost of 130 million rupees. It was built by two brothers, Vastupal and Tejpal, who were ministers of the Solanki king of Gujarat. They built it in the memory of their brother Luna. The temple is dedicated to the twenty-second TEERTHANKAR Neminath. The design of the temple is similar to Vimal Vasahi. There are 52 cells in the corridor surrounding the main sanctum. In the center of the dome of the grand hall (RANG MANDAP) hangs an exceptionally elaborate marble chandelier. Luna Vasahi was also destroyed by Ala-Uddin Khilji and the original idol of Neminath was mutilated. The temple was repaired in 1321 A.D. by Pethod, and a new idol of Neminath was installed.

Pitalhar Temple was built in 1315-1433 A.D. by Bhima Shah who was a minister of Sultan Begada of Ahmedabad. A beautiful metal idol of the first TEERTHANKAR Rishabhadev is installed in this temple. The statue is 8 ft high and 5.5 ft wide. It is cast from an alloy of five metals, mostly brass (PITAL), and weighs 4.4 tons. Khartar Vasahi is a temple dedicated to the twenty-third TEERTHANKAR Parshvanath. It was built by Mandalik and his family in 1458-59 A.D. It has three levels, and with its dome and steeple, it is the tallest structure in the Delwara Temple Complex. In the sanctum, on each of the four sides, marble idols of Bhagwaan Parshvanath are installed. Canopies of nine snake-hoods adorn the idols. The outer walls of the sanctum are decorated with figures of gods and goddesses, lamps and other objects carved in grey sandstone. The Temple of Mahaveer Swami is a small, simple structure built in 1582 A.D. dedicated to the last TEERTHANKAR of the current era.

Because of the architecture and beauty of the Delwara temples and their serene ambience, Jains consider Mount Abu to be an important place of pilgrimage similar to Palitana, Girinar, Sammed Shikhar and Shravanbelgola. About four miles from the Delwara temples, in Achalagarh, there are temples of Mahadev and Raghunathji, and Vashishthaashram.[1] So Mount Abu is a holy place for Hindus as well. On the way to Achalagarh there are three Jain temples, two dedicated to Bhagwaan Rishabhadev and one to the seventeenth TEERTHANKAR Kunthunath.

Like all places of pilgrimage, Mount Abu is very pleasant and enjoyable to visit. It reminds us of our rich heritage and provides an atmosphere to think of the pristine principles of Jainism.

---

1 Mahadev is another name of Bhagwaan Shiva, Raghunathji is a name of Bhagwaan Ram and Guru Vashishtha was Bhagwaan Ram's teacher.

## Learning Vows (शिक्षाव्रत)

Acharya Samant Bhadra, in RATNAKARAND SHRAAVAKAACHAAR, presents the following four learning vows:

1. Periodic limit on the field of activity (देशावकाशिक)
2. Practice of equanimity (सामायिक)
3. Partial or total fast (प्रोषधोपवास)
4. Service to the virtuous (वैय्यावृत्य)

By practicing the learning vows, a householder learns to gradually adopt the augmenting vows and to eventually embrace the conduct of a monk.

Four learning vows:

देशावकाशिकं वा, सामयिकं प्रोषधोपवासो वा ।
वैय्यावृत्यं शिक्षा-व्रतानि चत्वारि शिष्टानि ।91 ।

DESHAAVAKAASHIKAM VA, SAAMAYIKAM PROSHADHOPAVAASO VA
VAIYYAAVRITYAM SHIKHA-VRATAANI CHATVAARI SHISHTAANI

Periodic limit on the field of activity,
equanimity, partial or total fasts on occasions,
and service to the virtuous and worthy
are said to be the four learning vows.

Periodic limit on the field of activity (DESHAAVAKAASHIK):

देशावकाशिकं स्यात्, कालपरिच्छेदनेन देशस्य ।
प्रत्यहमणुव्रतानां, प्रतिसंहारो विशालस्य ।92 ।

DESHAAVAKAASHIKAM SYAAT, KAALAPARICHCHHEDANEN DESHASYA
PRATYAHAMANUVRATAANAAM, PRATISAMHAARO VISHAALASYA

A votary, who practices the partial vows and has taken
the vow of limiting one's field of activity, periodically
sets additional limits on one's field of activity, and thus
practices the learning vow of periodic limit on field of activity.

Limits of the field of activity:

गृहहारिग्रामाणां, क्षेत्रनदीदावयोजनानां च ।
देशावकाशिकस्य, स्मरन्ति सीम्नां तपोवृद्धाः ।93 ।

GRIHAHAARIGRAAMAANAAM, KSHETRANADEEDAAVAYOJANAANAAM CHA
DESHAAVAKAASHIKASYA, SMARANTI SEEMNA TAPOVRIDDHAH

The periodic limits on field of activity are set
by means of boundaries defined by distances or
by house, street, town, farm, river or forest.
This is the teaching of those who perform supreme penance.

Periods of limiting the field of activity:

सम्वत्सरमृतुरयनं, मासचतुर्मासपक्षमृक्षं च ।
देशावकाशिकस्य, प्राहुः कालावधिं प्राज्ञाः ।94 ।

SAMVATSARAMRITURAYANAM, MAASACHATURMAASAPAKSHAMRIKSHAM CHA
DESHAAVAKAASHIKASYA, PRAAHUH KAALAAVADHIM PRAAJNAAH

Periods of limiting one's field of activity are
a year, a season, six months, four months,
two months, a month, two weeks, a week, or a day.
The scholarly monks have described these details.

Practice of major vows outside the boundary:

सीमान्तानां परतः, स्थूलेतर पञ्चपापसन्त्यागात् ।
देशावकाशिकेन च, महाव्रतानि प्रसाध्यन्ते ।95 ।

SEEMAANTAANAAM PARATAH, STHOOLETAR PANCHAPAAPASANTYAAGAAT
DESHAAVAKAASHIKEN CHA, MAHAAVRITAANI PRASAADHYANTE

The votary who observes periodic limit on field of activity,
remains free from indulging in five undesirable activities,
such as violence, untruth and possessiveness, gross as well as subtle.
Hence he/she essentially practices the major vows outside the limit.

Transgressions of periodic limit on the field of activity:

प्रेषण शब्दानयने, रूपाभिव्यक्ति पुद्गलक्षेपौ ।
देशाविकाशिकस्य, व्यपदिश्यन्तेऽत्ययाः पञ्च ।96 ।

PRESHAN SHABDAANAYANE, ROOPAABHIVYAKTI PUDGALAKSHEPAU
DESHAAVAKAASHIKASYA, VYAPADISHYANTE-ATYAYAH PANCH

Sending others on errands, calling, displaying signs,
communicating through gestures, and sending materials;
such activities of body and speech constitute
the five transgressions of periodic limit on field of activity.

Practice of equanimity (SAAMAAYIK):

आसमयमुक्ति मुक्तं, पञ्चाघानामशेषभावेन ।
सर्वत्र च सामयिका, सामयिकं नाम शंसन्ति ।97 ।

AASAMAYAMUKTI MUKTAM, PANCHAAGHAANAAMASHESHABHAAVEN
SARVATRA CHA SAAMAYIKA, SAAMAYIKAM NAAM SHAMSANTI

A votary makes a firm resolve to totally abstain from
the five sins including violence, untruth and sensual pleasures,
through his activities, physical as well as mental, for a set period.
This is equanimity according to sages, spiritually elevated.

Periods of practice of equanimity:

मूर्धरुहमुष्टिवासो-बंधं पर्य्यङ्कबन्धनं चापि ।
स्थानमुपवेशनं वा, समयं जानन्ति समयज्ञाः ।98 ।

MOORDHARUHAMUSHTIVAASO-BANDHAM PARYYANKABANDHANAM CHAAPI
STHAANAMUPAVESHANAM VA, SAMAYAM JAANANTI SAMAYAJNAAH

The time limit for practice of equanimity is set willfully
by means of some physical event such as opening of the knot in hair
or clothes, comfort in maintaining a posture, sitting or standing.
This knowledge has been imparted by sagacious individuals.

Suitable places for practice of equanimity:

एकान्ते सामयिकं, निर्व्याक्षेपे वनेषु वास्तुषु च ।
चैत्यालयेषु वापि च, परिचेतव्यं प्रसन्नधिया ।99 ।

EKAANTE SAAMAYIKAM, NIRVYAAKSHEPE VANESHU VAASTUSHU CHA
CHAITYAALAYESHU VAAPI CHA, PARICHETAVYAM PRASANNADHIYA

An individual practicing equanimity, with cheerful state of mind,
selects an appropriate location for practice of equanimity,
a solitary place such as a park or forest, building, temple
or place of worship, where there is little chance of interruption.

Extending practice of equanimity:

व्यापार-वैमनस्या-द्विनिवृत्यामन्तरात्मविनिवृत्याम् ।
सामयिकं बध्नीया-दुपवासे चैकभुक्ते वा ।100 ।

VYAAPAAR-VAIMANSYA-DVINIVRITYAAMANTARAATMAVINIVRITYAAM
SAAMAYIKAM BADHNEEYA-DUPAVAASE CHAIKABHUKTE VA

On the days of observance of partial or total fast,
being free from physical and mental activities, and
abstaining from the activities of routine work and business,
one should reinforce the practice of equanimity.

Daily practice of equanimity:

सामयिकं प्रतिदिवसं, यथावदप्यनलसेन चेतव्यम् ।
व्रतपञ्चकपरिपूरण-कारणमवधान-युक्तेन ।101 ।

SAAMAYIKAM PRATIDIVASAM, YATHAAVADAPYANALASEN CHETAVYAM
VRATPANCHAKPARIPOORAN-KAARANAMAVADHAAN-YUKTEN

On other days too, a householder practices equanimity,
with conscience free from indolence, with concentration,
following a proper procedure; for practice of equanimity
complements the five vows such as nonviolence and truth.

Emulating a monk through practice of equanimity:

सामयिके सारम्भाः, परिग्रहा नैव सन्ति सर्वेऽपि ।
चेलोपसृष्टमुनिरिव, गृही तदा याति यतिभावम् ।102 ।

SAAMAYIKE SAARAMBHAAH, PARIGRAHA NAIV SANTI SARVEPI
CHELOPSRISTAMUNIRIV, GRIHI TADA YAATI YATIBHAAVAM

During the period of equanimity, a votary does not
indulge in work and business related mental activities.

Consequently, in spite of having material possessions,
a householder enjoys the mental state of a monk.

Performing like a monk during practice of equanimity:

शीतोष्णदंशमशक-परीषहमुपसर्गमपि च मौनधराः ।
सामयिकं प्रतिपन्ना, अधिकुर्वीरन्नचलयोगाः ।103 ।

SHEETOSHNADANSHAMASHAK-PAREESHAHAMUPASARGAMAPI CHA MAUNADHARAAH
SAAMAYIKAM PRATIPANNA, ADHIKURVEERANNACHALAYOGAAH

A votary performs like a monk during the practice of equanimity;
he/she refrains from reacting to heat and cold, stings of insects;
he/she does not mind any unexpected painful hardships;
a true practice of equanimity entails sereneness of mind as well.

Objects of contemplation during practice of equanimity:

अशरणमशुभमनित्यं, दुःखमनात्मानमावसामि भवम् ।
मोक्षस्तद्विपरीता-त्मेति ध्यायन्तु सामयिके ।104 ।

ASHARANAMASHUBHAMANITYAM, DUHKHAMANAATMAANAMAAVASAAMI BHAVAM
MOKSHASTADVIPAREETA-TMETI DHYAAYANTU SAAMAYIKE

Objects of contemplation during practice of equanimity are:
Inefficacy of others' endeavor (in spiritual advancement),
undesirable aspects and transient nature of worldly existence,
and that salvation is the opposite of painful, mundane life.

Transgressions of practice of equanimity:

वाक्कायमानसानां, दुःप्रणिधानान्यनादरस्मरणे ।
सामयिकस्यातिगमा, व्यज्यन्ते पञ्च भावेन ।105 ।

VAAKKAAYAMAANASAANAAM, DUHPRANIDHAANAANYANAADARASMARANE
SAAMAYIKASYAATIGAMA, VYAJYANTE PANCH BHAAVEN

Five transgressions of practice of equanimity include:
Indulgence in unwholesome activities of body, speech and mind,
disrespect for the practice of equanimity, and
forgetfulness of the recitation of prayers and verses.

The learning vow of partial or total fast (PROSHADHOPAVAAS):

पर्वण्यष्टम्यां च, ज्ञातव्यः प्रोषधोपवासस्तु ।
चतुरभ्यवहार्य्याणां, प्रत्याख्यानं सदेच्छाभिः ।106 ।

PARVANYASHTAMYAAM CHA, JNAATAVYAH PROSHADHOPAVAASASTU
CHATURABHYAVAHAARYYAANAAM, PRATYAAKHYAANAM SADECHCHHAABHIH

A votary, making a resolve with his/her own freewill,
abstains from taking four kinds of food on special days,
as the eighth and fourteenth days of each fortnight;
this is known as the vow of partial or total fast.

Method of observing partial or total fast:

पञ्चानां पापाना-मलङ्क्रिया-रम्भगन्धपुष्पाणाम् ।
स्नानाञ्जननस्याना-मुपवासे परिहृतिं कुर्य्यात् ।107 ।

PANCHAANAAM PAAPAANAAMALANKRIYAARAMBHAGANDHAPUSHPAANAAM
SNAANAANJANANASYAANAAMUPAVAASE PARIHRITIM KURYAAT

A votary does not indulge in business and household activities,
involving violence, untruth and the like, on the day of a fast;
does not wear fine clothes, ornaments, perfumes or garlands;
does not seek gratification in luxurious bath and cosmetics.

Religious activities during a partial or total fast:

धर्मामृतं सतृष्णः, श्रवणाभ्यां पिबतु पाययेद्वान्यान् ।
ज्ञानध्यानपरो वा, भवतूपवसन्नतन्द्रालुः ।108 ।

DHARMAAMRITAM SATRISHNAH, SHRAVANAABHYAAM PIBATU PAAYAYEDWAANYAAN
JNAANADHYAANAPARO VA, BHAVATOOPVASANNATANDRAALUH

A person, observing a fast, does not remain idle;
being enthusiastic to drink the nectar of religious knowledge,
he/she enjoys religious discourses and participates in discussions;
thus he/she spends the day seeking knowledge and in meditation.

Kinds of fasts:

चतुराहारविसर्जन-मुपवासः प्रोषधः सकृद्भुक्तिः ।
सः प्रोषधोपवासो, यदुपोष्यारम्भमाचरति ।109 ।

CHATURAAHAARAVISARJANAMUPVAASAH PROSHADHAH SAKRIDBHUKTIH
SAH PROSHADHOPAVAASO, YADUPOSHYAARAMBHAMAACHARATI

During the period of twenty-four hours,
abstaining from four kinds of food is total fast;
eating only once is called partial fast; and a total fast
preceded and followed by partial fasts is an extended fast.

Transgressions of the learning vow of partial or total fast:

ग्रहणविसर्गास्तरण-न्यदृष्टमृष्टान्यनादरस्मरणे ।
यत्प्रोषधोपवास व्यतिलङ्घनपञ्चकं तदिदम् ।110 ।

GRAHANVISARGAASTARANANYADRISHTAMRISHTAANAYANAADARASMARANE
YATPROSHADHOPAVAAS VYATILANGHAN PANCHAKAM TADIDAM

The transgressions of partial, total and extended fasts are:
incautiously picking up and putting down utensils, bedding
and other materials; lack of respect for essential duties,
and not being conscientious of proper procedures and activities.

The learning vow of service to the worthy (VAIYAAVRITYA):

दानं वैयावृत्यं, धर्माय तपोधनाय गुणनिधये ।
अनपेक्षितोपचारो-पक्रियमगृहाय विभवेन ।111 ।

DAANAM VAIYAAVRITYAM, DHARMAAYA TAPODHANAAYA GUNANIDHAYE
ANAPEKSHITOPACHAAROPAKRIYAMAGRIHAAYA VIBHAVEN

Offering food, medicine and literature, not for gaining name or fame,
to estimable monks, who have renounced their households,

for promoting their penance and spiritual advancement,
and for similar advancement of self, is called service to the worthy.

Another aspect of service to the worthy:

व्यापत्तिव्यपनोदः, पदयोः सम्वाहनं च गुणरागात् ।
वैयावृत्यं यावा-नुपग्रहोऽन्योऽपि संयमिनाम् ।112 ।

VYAAPATTIVYAPANODAH, PADAYOH SAMVAAHANAM CHA GUNARAAGAAT
VAIYAAVRITYAM YAAVAANUPAGRAHOANYOAPI SAMYAMINAAM

Another aspect of service to the worthy includes
relieving their physical pain through massage and medicine,
and helping them in their spiritual pursuit in all possible ways.
A votary performs such services merely for his love of virtues.

Mode of offering materials to the worthy:

नवपुण्यैः प्रतिपत्तिः, सप्तगुणसमाहितेन शुद्धेन ।
अपसूनारम्भाणा-मार्याणामिष्यते दानम् ।113 ।

NAVAPUNYAIH PRATIPATTIH, SAPTAGUNASAMAAHITEN SHUDDHEN
APASOONAARAMBHAANAAMAARYAANAAMISHYATE DAANAM

A householder having seven qualities[1] donates to monks,
who have renounced their families and households,
food, medicine and books, with due respect
by following the prescribed rules and procedures.

Advantages of service to the worthy:

गृहकर्मणापिनिचितं, कर्म विमार्ष्टि खलु गृहविमुक्तानाम् ।
अतिथीनां प्रतिपूजा, रुधिरमलं धावते वारि ।114 ।

GRIHAKARMANAAPINICHITAM, KARMA VIMAARSHTI KHALU GRIHAVIMUKTAANAAM
ATITHEENAAM PRATIPOOJA, RUDHIRAMALAM DHAAVATE VAARI

A genuine service to the worthy personalities,
consisting of the offering of food and other materials,
mitigates the demerit of thoughts and feelings of the donor,
just as water washes away a spot of blood.

Influx of beneficial karma:

उच्चैर्गोत्रं प्रणते-र्भोगो दानादुपासनात्पूजा ।
भक्तेः सुन्दररूपं, स्तवनात्कीर्तिस्तपोनिधिषु ।115 ।

UCHCHAIRGOTRAM PRANATE-BHOGO DAANAADUPAASANATPOOJA
BHAKTE SUNDARAROOPAM, STAVANAATKEERTISTAPONIDHISHU

(Though the service to the worthy involves no desires,)
a householder, by praising and worshiping virtuous monks,
who perform penance for spiritual advancement,
acquires good status-determining and physique-determining karmas.

---

1 Presented in Lesson 36.

Inception of spiritual progress:

क्षितिगतमिव वटबीजं, पात्रगतं दानमल्पमपि काले ।
फलतिच्छायाविभवं, बहुफलमिष्टं शरीरभृताम् ।116 ।

KSHITIGATAMIV VATABEEJAM, PAATRAGATAM DAANAMALPAMAPI KAALE
FALATICHCHHAAYAAVIBHAVAM, BAHUFALAMISHTAM SHAREERABHRITAAM

A little donation to the worthy, properly administered,
in due course, leads to considerable merit for individuals,
just as a large shady tree develops from a small seed,
that is thoughtfully sown in fertile ground.

Four kinds of charity:

आहारौषधयोर-प्युपकरणावासयोश्च दानेन ।
वैयावृत्यं ब्रुवते, चतुरात्मत्वेन चतुरस्त्राः ।117 ।

AAHAARAUSHADHAYORAPYUPAKARANAAVAASAYOSHCHA DAANEN
VAIYAAVRITYAM BRUVATE, CHATURAATMATVEN CHATURASRAAH

Those who possess four kinds of knowledge
have prescribed four kinds of service to the worthy:
Providing food, medicine, shelter and books
which are necessary for enhancing one's spiritual knowledge.

An aspect of service to the worthy - worship of VEETARAAG:

देवाधिदेवचरणे, परिचरणं सर्वदुःखनिर्हरणम् ।
कामदुहि कामदाहिनि, परिचिनुयादादृतो नित्यम् ।118 ।

DEVAADHIDEVACHARANE, PARICHARANAM SARVADUHKHANIRHARANAM
KAAMADUHI KAAMADAAHINI, PARICHINUYAADAADRITO NITYAM

Worship of VEETARAAGs – who are without attachment and aversion,
with the resolve to follow in their footsteps, leads to spiritual uplift,
alleviates the desire for worldly pleasures and relieves suffering;
such worship, performed daily, is an aspect of service to the worthy.

Transgressions of the learning vow of service to the worthy:

हरितपिधाननिधाने-ह्यनादरास्मरणमत्सरत्वानि ।
वैयावृत्यस्यैते, व्यतिक्रमाः पञ्च कथ्यन्ते ।121 ।

HARITAPIDHAANANIDHAANEDYANADARAASMARANAMATSARATVAANI
VAIYAAVRITYASYAITE, VYATIKRAMAAH PANCH KATHYANTE

(Far more organisms are present on green leaves than on other utensils;)
thus using green leaves for storing and covering food and other things,
lack of respect for the acceptor, forgetfulness and envy
constitute the transgressions of the vow of service to the worthy.

The learning vows constitute an important part of rational conduct for householders.

## Path To Liberation: A Prayer

English adaptation of Budhjan's "PRABHU PATIT PAAWAN"
by Shri Girdhar Lal Jain

O Prabhu,[1] I am an impure worldly soul
and you have broken the cycle of birth and rebirth,
and have revealed the path to liberation,
I perceive this character of yours,
so I have resolved to follow in your footsteps.

So far, before discerning your qualities,
I sought the help of various gods and goddesses,
I failed to apply my intellect to understand the self
and mistook delusion to be auspicious.

In the thick jungle of worldly existence, karma,
my enemy, robbed me of my wealth of knowledge,
hence I lost my sense of direction;
and forgetting my auspicious goal, I took inauspicious paths.

This is the auspicious moment,
this is the auspicious day,
this is my auspicious life,
my fortunes have risen,
I have visualized your characteristics, O Prabhu.

You are beyond attachment and aversion;
you are the embodiment of non-possessiveness;
your image shows you in deep meditation;
displaying eight external adornments,
your qualities are infinite;
they surpass the brilliance of millions of suns.

---

1 The word ' PRABHU ' means venerable in this context.

My dark delusion has been removed,
the sun of self-realization has risen in my soul,
my heart has been filled with real joy,
the joy of a poor man who finds a precious stone
that will fulfill all his needs.

With folded hands, I bow my head,
I express my devotion to your footprints;
you are supreme, the most eminent in the universe;
I pray to you, the exponent of the path to liberation.

I have no desire for heaven,
I have no desire for any kingdom
or for the company of friends and relatives,
I, 'Budh', wish for the devotion to your virtues,
until I attain salvation, the most auspicious state.

* * * * * * *

## Aristotle's Concept of God

God has no physical form. Thus He does not feel pain, hunger, thirst and desire. God is pure knowledge. Knowing is His one and only activity.

God possesses the knowledge of each and everything inherently and continually. He has no function except self-realization. If some other function is attributed to God, some goal or purpose, aside from Him, will have to be assumed. Thereby God will have the blemish of limitedness and finiteness.

In this respect, Aristotle's God is similar to the God of Jains.

- Babu Gulabrai M. A.

* * * * * * *

31

## Truth Succeeds: A Moral Story[1]

Once upon a time, in a small town in India, there lived two friends, Sameer and Sanjay. They were partners in business. They did not do anything without consulting each other. Their business was flourishing.

One year the business was very profitable so they decided to invest some of their profits in gold. They bought gold bars and put them in their safe. Only Sameer and Sanjay knew the combination of the safe. So they felt very secure.

Both friends had dreams of becoming richer by selling the gold at a higher price. However, Sameer became impatient. He did not want to wait for the price to go up. He devised a scheme to defraud his partner. While Sanjay was out of town, Sameer removed the gold from the safe and put charcoal in its place.

When Sanjay returned, Sameer said, "Let us check the gold in the safe to see that everything is alright." Sanjay agreed. When the safe was opened, they found pieces of charcoal in place of gold. Sameer pretended to be surprised. He said, "How sad! The gold has turned into charcoal. We are ruined. We will have to dissolve our partnership but we will remain good friends and help each other."

Sanjay understood the whole story. He realized that his friend had replaced the gold with charcoal during his absence. However, he did not argue with Sameer who had deceived him. Even though he knew it would be difficult to get his fair share, Sanjay did not give up hope.

Sanjay devised a plan to teach his friend a lesson. He made a life-size statue of Sameer and trained two small monkeys to play with the statue. When the monkeys were given food of their choice, they would sit on the shoulders of the statue and eat the food.

One day, Sanjay invited his friends and relatives to a dinner party. Sameer and his family were also invited. As usual, Sameer's wife Seema came a few hours before the party to help. Their two young sons, Apoorva and Anil, accompanied her.

The guests arrived and the party started. The children were served food in a separate room. The dinner was over before sunset.

---

[1] Based on a moral story from 'Seven Pearls Of Wisdom' by Dr. Jagadishchandra Jain, 1984.

Everybody enjoyed the delicious dinner. After the dinner, Sanjay had arranged a program of music and dance. People were waiting for the program to begin. However, Sameer felt rather uneasy since he had a guilty conscience. He could not get over the thought that he had deceived his good friend Sanjay who was respected by everyone in the town. He said to Sanjay, "My friend, the dinner was delicious and I enjoyed the party. But I have to leave early because I have another commitment. Will you please call my sons from the other room?"

Sanjay arranged to bring the two monkeys to the party room and gave them some food. The monkeys immediately jumped onto Sameer's shoulders and began to enjoy the food. All eyes were fixed on them. Sameer was at a loss to understand the situation. He angrily asked Sanjay, "What is this? You have insulted me before everyone."

Sanjay said aloud, "My dear friend, you asked me to call your sons, Apoorva and Anil. I have fulfilled your wishes. Apoorva and Anil are sitting on your shoulders. You did not recognize them but they know you very well."

Sameer said, "These are not my sons. They are monkeys. What is this nonsense?"

Sanjay said, "Sameer, your sons turned into monkeys this afternoon while playing with my children."

Sameer said, "How can human beings turn into monkeys? It is impossible."

Sanjay replied, "Human beings can turn into monkeys just like gold in our safe turned into charcoal. Don't you remember?"

Sameer realized his mistake. He felt shamed. He admitted what he had done. He said, "Sanjay, you have made me realize my mistake. I am very sorry. I will give you your share of gold which I took from the safe."

The two friends became partners in business again.

The Adeeshwar Bhagwaan Temple
Shatrunjaya Hills

## Shatrunjaya (Palitana)

by Richa A. Jain and Sunita Jain

Like other religions, Jainism has several places of pilgrimage, called TEERTH. Some of the prominent ones are Sammed Shikhar (in Bihar), Girnar (in Gujarat), Shatrunjaya (in Gujarat), Mount Abu (in Rajasthan) and Pavapuri (in Bihar).

Shatrunjaya, one of the most important Jain TEERTHs, is located on a hill two miles to the south of Palitana, a small town in Gujarat. It is believed that many great souls attained salvation (MOKSHA) at Shatrunjaya by shedding their karma, the enemies (SHATRUs) or hindrance to spiritual progress. Hence the name Shatrunjaya. It is believed that Pundareek, the chief interpreter (GANADHAR) of Bhagwaan Adinath[1] attained salvation at Shatrunjaya. Thus it is also called Pundareek. According to Jain literature, the five Pandava brothers – Yudhishthir, Bheem, Arjun, Nakul and Sahdev, also performed penance here and attained salvation.

Shatrunjaya (Palitana) is called the 'City of Temples.' Writing about this place of pilgrimage, the well-known archaeologist, P. C. Dasgupta, writes,[2] "The splendor of architecture as a crowning achievement of taste and inspiration for the realization of eternity has been seldom reflected as it is amidst the profound panorama of Shatrunjaya famed for its city of nearly a thousand temples."

Shatrunjaya Hills rise 2000 feet above sea level. There are two principal peaks covered with beautifully sculpted and magnificently decorated temples. Some temples are believed to have been constructed in the 11th century. However, most were built in the 15th century. Momentous development of Shatrunjaya took place during the Solanki era. King Kumarpal Solanki, a disciple of the great Acharya Hemchandra, was mainly responsible for the expansion and renovation of the ancient temples. Since the Solanki era, several other temples have been built at Shatrunjaya. At present, there are

1 The first TEERTHANKAR, Bhagwaan Rishabhadev is also called Adinath or Adeeshwar.

2 Introduction of the book 'The Temples of Satrunjaya' by James Burgess, published by Jain Bhawan, Calcutta 1977.

almost 4000 Jain temples, big and small, spread over the Shatrunjaya Hills.

From Palitana, a broad, tree-lined road leads to the foot of the mountain. The ascent begins with a wide flight of steps guarded on either side by statues of elephants. In this area there are several miniature temples with CHARANs – marble slabs carved in *bas relief* showing a representation of Arihant's feet.[3] The winding path leading upward is occasionally interrupted by regular steps. The ascent gets steep at several points. For the convenience of pilgrims, at frequent intervals, there are many reservoirs of water (KUNDs) and wells (BAOLIs), rest houses and water fountains along the path.

A little way up the hill is a small rest area rendered sacred by the PAADUKAs (SANDALs) of Bharat, the eldest son of Bhagwaan Adinath. Further up is a fountain called ICCHA sanctified by the PAADUKAs of Bhagwaan Neminath. Almost halfway up the hill, there is a large rest area called SHILA KUND named after its reservoir and surrounded by a small garden. Still further up is the sacred Hindu site (STHAAN) of the six sons of Devaki. The temple has representations of the six infants in black marble. Up near the top of the hill is the temple of the Hindu deity, Hanuman. At this point the path bifurcates, the path on the right leads to the northern peak and the path on the left leads to the southern peak.

Ascending toward the northern peak the path passes through a narrow door into an outer enclosure. In the left corner of this area, under a tree, there is the shrine (DARGAAH) of Hengar, a Muslim holy personality (PEER). Legend goes that Hengar tried to strike Adinath's idol with his war club, but instead, he lost his life. The view of the surrounding area from this point is breathtaking. Toward the north, surrounded by clumps of trees, is the town of Palitana, and beyond it lies the granite range of Sihor. Toward the west, in the far distance, lies Mount Girnar. In all other directions spreads a vast plane with dips and rises, dotted with little villages and areas of cultivated land. The Shatrunjaya river winds like a silver ribbon across the foreground losing itself between the Talaja and Khokara hills in the

3 In Jain tradition, we worship CHARANs as a reminder of the path to salvation exemplified by ARIHANTs, the worthy. While worshiping the CHARANs, we make a resolve to follow in the footsteps of ARIHANTs.
- D. C. J.

southwest.

The view nearby is no less awe-inspiring – thousands of intricately sculpted temples built of stone and marble sprawled over the entire mountain, the paths winding around them populated not only by worshipers but also by squirrels, doves, pigeons and occasionally even peacocks.

Like other holy places, Shatrunjaya has its narrative of glory (MAHAATMYA), which distinguishes it as a great place of pilgrimage. This text is one of the oldest known Jain documents, dating as far back as 420 A.D. It was composed by Dhaneshvar of Valabhi at the request of Shiladitya, the king of Saurashtra at that time. It is a long panegyric in Sanskrit running to about 8700 lines. It is believed to be the legend of this mountain as told by Bhagwaan Mahaveer upon Indra's request. It presents the story of the mountain interwoven with episodes from Hindu mythology. According to legend, the hill has a hundred and eight names and as many peaks called TONKs.

Shatrunjaya temples are named after the idols enshrined within or the individual who built them. The walls of most temples present scenes from stories and legends. The outside of each temple is elaborately decorated. The temples vary in size and architecture and represent the variations of style over the ages.

A notable feature of Shatrunjaya is the colossal, 18 foot high sitting idol of Bhagwaan Adinath (also called Adibuddha, Bhima Padam or Bhima Pandava). It is carved out of solid rock on the northern summit and measures 14 feet from knee to knee. It is enclosed in a low-domed temple of comparatively recent construction. The HATHI POLE or Elephant gate is named after the two elephants created in *bas relief* in plaster on both sides of the gate that leads to the temple of MULANAYAK (the principal idolized personality) Adeeshwar Bhagwaan which is on the Vimalavasi Tonk. The main structure is surrounded by many little cells or sanctums, which seem to have been added later. The idol of Bhagwaan Adeeshwar in the sanctum is very large, with crystal eyes, a golden necklace, bracelets and a crown. There are numerous other statues in the temple, including fifty-five small statues in the main sanctum. Altogether the temple has two hundred and seventy-four objects of worship, including the idols of Rishabhadev's parents, Nabhiraya and Marudevi, seated on two marble elephants, images of Gautam Swami, Mahalakshmi, two ascetics (TAPASVIs) and a couple (JUGALIA, a male and female who are supposed to have been born, lived and died together).

Of all the temples on the Vimalavasi Tonk, the BHULAONI (labyrinth) is one of the older ones. It was completed in the early 15th century. It has a double row of small spires. Parts of the temple may have been built at different times, some dating back to the 12th or 13th century. Another temple on this tonk, dedicated to Bhagwaan Adinath, contains, among other objects of worship, a KSHETRAPAL (protector) and a YANTRA (an auspicious drawing on a sheet of copper).

The CHAUMUKH (four-sided) temple is the principal temple on the Kharataravasi Tonk. In this temple four images of a TEERTHANKAR are seated back to back so as to face the four cardinal points.

The Motisha temple is one of many temples in the valley, constructed in the early 18th century. The arch over its entrance is decorated by a carved double bracket (TORAN) with two figures of gatekeepers (DWAARAPAALs).

The inscriptions in the vestibule of the temple of Adeeshwar Bhagwaan aptly describe Shatrunjaya as the choicest of all hills, resembling the golden hill of MERU (a mountain in Jain mythology), with trees like the KALPAVRIKSHA (a mythological tree that is believed to fulfill all wishes).

Shatrunjaya is a place of pilgrimage where one can go for peace of mind and to uplift one's spirit. It also provides important information about the history of Jainism through some of its ancient inscriptions.

*Bibliography:*

1. The Temples of Satrunjaya by James Burgess, published by Jain Bhawan, Calcutta 1977.
2. JAIN TEERTH DARSHAN (Hindi) edited by Akshaya Kumar Jain, Radhe Shyam 'Pragalbh' and Shiv Nath Mittal, published by A. B. D. Jain Parishad Publishing House, Delhi, 1981.
3. CHARITRA NIRMAAN, volume three (Hindi) by Pandit Ugra Sen Jain, published by A. B. D. Jain Parishad Publishing House, Delhi, 1983.

# The Story of Chandana[1]

by Dr. Nemi Chandra Shastri Jyotishacharya

The story of Chandana is a vivid illustration of the consequences of karma and pseudo-karma (NOKARMA) on the lives of worldly souls. It also exemplifies the effects of vices such as lust, greed and misunderstanding that we routinely encounter in our lives. Further, it shows that in many instances, we suffer on account of circumstances that are beyond our control. Slightly different versions of the story conveying essentially similar messages appear in the Jain literature. - D. C. J.

## Early Life

Chandana was born a princess. She was the youngest among her siblings. Her sisters were married into royal families. They enjoyed palatial abodes and beds of roses. Chandana's life, on the other hand, took many strange turns. She encountered considerable pain and suffering in her life.

The early life of Chandana was majestic. Because of her beauty and grace, she was the jewel of her father's kingdom. Chandana's serene beauty, golden complexion and slim physique attracted everyone's attention. Through her unparalleled grace and charm, Chandana won the admiration of all.

## Kidnapping

It was springtime. The royal garden was in full bloom. Honey bees were humming and dancing from flower to flower. Chandana was enjoying a stroll in the garden, singing softly in her sweet, melodious voice.

As Chandana was walking along, a VIDHYADHAR[2] caught sight of

---

1 English adaptation based on the book TEERTHANKAR MAHAVEER AUR UNKI ACHARYA PARAMPARA, published by Jain Vidwat Parishad, Sagar, M.P., India, 1974, volume 1, pages 168-172.
Chandana is also known as MAHASATI Chandanbala. The word MAHASATI implies a lady of impeccable character.

2 The Sanskrit word VIDHYADHAR literally means one who is proficient in various arts and crafts. Possibly the VIDHYADHAR who noticed Chandana was an illusionist.

her. He was enchanted by Chandana's beauty and melodious voice. Chandana took possession of his heart and mind. He kidnapped Chandana. She tried to escape but to no avail.

Chandana cried for help. She slashed herself with her nails and wept but the VIDHYADHAR did not let go of her. He was bent on taking advantage of Chandana while she was struggling to protect her innocence. By chance, the VIDHYADHAR's wife passed that way. The VIDHYADHAR was afraid that his wife might discover his misdeed. So he took Chandana to a wild forest and left her there.

### Captivity

Poor Chandana wandered through the frightful jungle helplessly. There were wild animals all around. She was hungry and thirsty. As Chandana wandered through the jungle, a tribesman saw her. The tribesman was struck by Chandana's beauty and charm. He had never seen such a beautiful woman. He could not believe that a human could have such stunning beauty. Thinking that Chandana was not human but a fairy or a goddess, he captured her and presented her to his chief.

On seeing Chandana, the tribal chief's mind was taken over by lust. He tried to convince Chandana to marry him but she refused to accept his proposition. She was a young woman of immaculate character and firm resolve. The tribal chief also did not give up easily. He subjected Chandana to all kinds of threats and torture, but Chandana remained true to her resolve and did not surrender to his demands.

When the tribal chief found that Chandana had remained firm in her resolve in spite of the torture, he realized that Chandana had inimitable strength of character. Chandana would rather die than succumb to his evil desires. So he decided to make some money by selling her.

### Auction

The tribal chief took Chandana to the market in the city of Kaushambi where he put her up for auction. People started bidding for Chandana. Just then, Vrishabhadatt, the wealthiest man in the city of Kaushambi, passed by. When he saw Chandana, his heart was filled with virtuous affection for her. He felt as if Chandana was his own daughter. He immediately raised the bid and brought Chandana home.

### Evil Spirit of Suspicion

Vrishabhadatt had a pure heart and noble mind. He treated Chandana as his own daughter. However, his wife Subhadra became suspicious because of Chandana's beauty and charm. She was afraid that Vrishabhadatt would ignore her and marry Chandana. She became apprehensive of facing this indignity. Once more, Chandana's beauty brought misery and suffering in her life. Subhadra started to treat Chandana like a slave girl. She would pass offensive remarks, subject Chandana to verbal abuse and hurt her feelings. But Chandana was helpless and stayed at Vrishabhadatt's home. She endured everything calmly. She believed that her plight was the consequence of her karma and pseudo-karma.

Time passed and Chandana attained maturity. Her beauty and charm bloomed. Subhadra's suspicion also deepened.

### More Suffering

One hot afternoon, Vrishabhadatt came home. While Chandana was helping him wash his feet, her long flowing hair slipped and covered her face. Vrishabhadatt affectionately helped her with the hair. His wife Subhadra saw the whole incident. Her suspicion increased. The thought that her husband had his eyes on Chandana became rooted in her mind. Subhadra decided to disfigure Chandana. But she could not succeed in her designs while her husband was in town.

Finally, Subhadra got the opportunity when Vrishabhadatt went out of town. Subhadra called a barber and had Chandana's head shaved. Chandana's long, luxurious, ornate hair that significantly enhanced her beauty was gone. Then Subhadra chained Chandana's feet and put her in the cellar. Chandana suffered untold misery. She began counting her days.

When Vrishabhadatt returned and did not see Chandana, a variety of misgivings appeared in his mind. He asked the servants and maids of the household but no one dared to reveal Chandana's whereabouts. On repeated questioning, one maid told the entire story. Vrishabhadatt went to the cellar where Chandana was locked. He was filled with sorrow. Her plight brought tears to his eyes. He sent for a blacksmith to cut Chandana's chains and free her from captivity.

### End of Suffering

At that time, Teerthankar Mahaveer was a monk. He had not yet attained omniscience (KEVAL JNAAN). He was performing austere penance and meditation in search of absolute truth. On account of a stringent resolve (ABHIGRAH) about accepting food,[3] Mahaveer had gone without food for six months. That day, Mahaveer happened to pass by Vrishabhadatt's house – a mere coincidence. The door to the cellar was open. Subhadra had sent some simple coarse food consisting of lentils for Chandana. When Chandana saw Mahaveer, she offered the food to him but he did not seem to stop. Chandana was disappointed and tears filled her eyes. The tears in Chandana's eyes, satisfied Mahaveer's resolve and he accepted the food. People watched in surprise. Mahaveer had not accepted the sumptuous food offered by various people for six months. He graciously accepted the simple food offered by Chandana.

The chains were cut and Chandana was freed. Her adopted father, Vrishabhadatt was happy. Her adopted mother, Subhadra, was remorseful and apologized for her misunderstanding and misdeeds. The people of Kaushambi celebrated the end of Chandana's misery.

Later, Chandana renounced the world and became a preeminent nun among Bhagwaan Mahaveer's followers.

---

3 Customarily, when a Jain monk goes out for food, he makes a resolve (अभिग्रह ABHIGRAH, प्रतिज्ञा PRATIJNA). Normally, the resolves are: he will accept food if a couple invites him; or if a man holding a jug invites him; or two ladies, one holding a jug and the other holding a plate, invite him. If the resolve is not satisfied, the monk may give up his resolve the following day and make a new one. Some of the resolves are quite elaborate and stringent. This is part of the code of conduct of Jain monks. In the present instance, Teerthankar Mahaveer had resolved that he will accept food from a young woman in chains with shaved head and tears in her eyes. Many followers and devotees offered food to Mahaveer but he had not accepted their offers. Further, he had not changed his resolve for six months.

# Relevance Of Jainism In Modern Times

by Duli Chandra Jain and Sunita Jain

Q: What makes Jainism relevant in modern times?

A: Jainism believes in the complete independence of each individual. Further, it teaches that self-help is the means of achieving such independence. Jainism is a religion which gives us independence even from God, all gods and goddesses.

Q: Does it imply that we have the freedom to believe in whatever we like and do whatever we please?

A: We Jains believe that only an omniscient (KEVALI) knows the absolute truth. This implies that we can not know the absolute truth. We study the scriptures that convey the thoughts of omniscients about how to achieve complete independence. We observe and experience what is around us. Based on these, we form our own concepts about life. We decide what we should do and what we should avoid. Thus we develop our own concept of religion and its practice.

Q: This implies that each individual is entitled to form his/her own concept of religion. How can we do that? We may not have enough knowledge about religion.

A: One important fact about Jainism is its simplicity.[1] Many religious scholars claim that some 'supernatural' element is an integral aspect of religion, which is beyond the grasp of the masses. But Jainism entails no supernatural element or mysticism. Bhagwaan Mahaveer's discourses were in the language of the masses and were understood by all. To learn about Jainism, we simply have to study, observe and experience.

Q: We hear the words such as 'vibrations', 'science of healing' and 'energy centers'. What is the significance of these in Jainism?

A: These concepts border on parapsychology and have very little to do with Jainism. They do not relate to the principles of Jainism.

Q: Some Jain teachers mention the 'power' of NAMOKAAR MANTRA. What is NAMOKAAR MANTRA?

A: NAMOKAAR MANTRA is a prayer of supreme human virtues. By reciting NAMOKAAR MANTRA, we are reminded of the good deeds and

---

1 "Some Features of The Jain Religion" by Prof. Shri Krishna Saksena, Jain Study Circular, Volume 10, October 1989, pages 3-10.

qualities of supreme human beings (ARIHANTs), of supreme souls (SIDDHAs), and, of the scholarly monks who preach (ACHARYAs, UPADHYAYAs and SADHUs). We think of the virtue of being beyond attachment and aversion (VEETRAAG). We have pure thoughts and good feelings. All prayers and worships in Jainism are performed for the same purpose. There is no mystical or supernatural element in any Jain religious practice.

Q: How can the different concepts of religion, developed by several individuals, all be true?

A: According to Jainism, one individual's concept of religion is as valid and appropriate as any other person's concept of religion. Further, our concept of religion changes as we grow and acquire more knowledge and experience.

Q: How is that possible? How can the concepts written in a holy book like the Bhagwat Gita or the Bible change according to an individual's perception?

A: Jainism says that the absolute truth, though known to the omniscient, can not be expressed in words, written or spoken. This is an important feature of the Jain religion. Jainism teaches us to believe in reality which is essentially what we observe and experience. It emphasizes that we should not lose sight of reality. We should also understand that our concept of reality changes with age, environment, experience and knowledge. For example, consider the item 'FATHER' that was published in a Dutch magazine:

4 Years: My Daddy can do anything.
7 Years: My Dad knows a lot, a whole lot.
8 Years: My Father doesn't know quite everything.
12 Years: Oh, well, naturally Father doesn't know that either.
14 Years: Father? Hopelessly old-fashioned.
21 Years: Oh, that man is out of date. What did you expect?
25 Years: He knows a little bit about it, but not much.
30 Years: Maybe we ought to find out what Dad thinks.
35 Years: A little patience. Let's get Dad's assessment before we do anything.
50 Years: I wonder what Dad would have thought about that. He was pretty smart.
60 Years: My Dad knew absolutely everything!
65 Years: I'd give anything if Dad were here so I could talk this over with him. I really miss that man.

It should be emphasized that the basic tenets of religion do not change, but our outlook, our understanding and our interpretation of religion evolve as our experience and knowledge expand.

Q: Does the Jain concept of individual freedom imply that we have the freedom to do whatever we wish?

A: We have to bear in mind that freedom imposes an important responsibility on us. My freedom should not infringe on the rights of other individuals. My freedom should not interfere with the right of other animals to survive. My thoughts, speech and actions should not hurt others' feelings. Otherwise, I would be committing violence. Our words and deeds should be such that we minimize the violence of others' feelings. All of us, adults as well as youngsters, should make a sincere effort to minimize the violence of each others' feelings. This will generate trust among us. Then the problems of generation gap, of communication, of growing up in a multicultural environment, will have a minimal untoward impact on our well-being. We have to have faith in our youngsters and our youngsters should have similar faith in us. This belief in nonviolence will produce harmony, happiness and peace of mind in families and in society. We should also remember that we are all human and we are apt to make honest mistakes of judgement.

Q: People use phrases like 'traditional versus new values', 'Western versus old Eastern orthodox', 'society that is morally different from Indian'. Are not these realities of present times?

A: Regardless of these slogans, all cultures teach the same morality. Physical and mental violence, untruth, greed and the like are deemed immoral in any system, old or new, Western or Eastern.

Q: Jainism says that the ultimate goal of each individual soul is salvation – freedom from the bondage of karma. Does this imply that we should renounce all worldly pursuits and follow the path to spiritual progress?

A: Jain sages have divided the society into four segments: Monks (SADHUs), nuns (SADHVIs), laymen (SHRAAVAKs) and laywomen (SHRAAVIKAs). Monks and nuns follow the path to spiritual development to a greater extent than householders. Nevertheless, householders are an essential component of society. All members of society are expected to fulfill their responsibilities towards each other with the best of their abilities. This is beneficial for all.

Q: If everybody followed the Jain teaching of non-possessiveness (APARIGRAH), how could modern science and technology develop?

A: As Jainism supports the concept of freedom of all individuals, it also supports the ideal of the prosperity of all individuals of the world. It does not prevent us from making progress in the fields of science and technology for the benefit of all people of the world. In TATTVARTHA SUTRA, Acharya Umaswati has written:

PARASPAROPAGRAHO JEEVAANAM:5-21:

The role of all living beings of the universe is to help each other. We must endeavor to help all of humanity. Dr. A. N. Upadhye has written[2], "The second virtue which Jain ethics lays stress on is good neighborliness. One should speak the truth and respect the right to property. Thus one becomes trustworthy of society, and at the same time creates an atmosphere of security for others. One's thoughts, words and acts must be consistent with each other. Further, they must create an atmosphere of confidence. A reciprocal sense of security must start with the immediate neighbor and then be gradually diffused in society at large, not only in theory but also in practice. These virtues can lead to coherent social and political groups of worthy citizens who yearn for peaceful coexistence with the well-being of the entire humanity in view." Thus the Jain teachings do not impede progress. Our concept of non-possessiveness (APARIGRAH) entails that in our endeavors, we do not look for our own interest only. We should consider the overall impact of our actions on the environment, including all living and non-living entities.

Q: Does it mean that we can accumulate a lot of material wealth?

A: It depends upon how the wealth is accumulated. Jainism teaches us to minimize physical and mental violence. It says that we should not indulge in passions such as greed, intrigue, untruth, ego and pride. We should not mislead or exploit others. We should bear in mind that virtues like nonviolence, truth and forthrightness bring mental peace and happiness. If our pursuit of materials leads to physical or mental suffering, or if it causes us to lose our peace of mind, it becomes violence. Thus we have to strike a balance between our mental happiness and the pursuit of money and material. In businesses and jobs, we should be impelled by the

2 'Mahavira And His Philosophy Of Life', included in Lord Mahavira And His Teachings, published by Shree Vallabhsuri Smarak Nidhi, Bombay, India, 1983.

desire to help our fellow beings. We should work for the good of all people. This is the kind of sacrifice our culture of nonviolence entails.

Q: What if one makes a considerable amount of money and donates a portion of it for worthy causes? Is it not APARIGRAH?

A: According to the Jain theory of karma, it is our thoughts, feelings and passions which lead to the influx of good or bad karma. If one indulges in greed, untruth, intrigue and deception in making money, one acquires bad karma (PAAP). Obviously, the consequences of such karma can not be avoided merely by donating some money. Further, donations made for name and fame do not bring any good karma (PUNYA).

Q: What are PAAP and PUNYA according to Jainism?

A: PAAP is the influx of harmful karma which takes place when we have undesirable feelings and thoughts, and PUNYA is the influx of beneficial karma which is caused by good thoughts and feelings.[3]

Q: Do we obtain wealth and other worldly possessions as consequences of our past good karma?

A: There is no role of karma in our obtaining any material possessions.[4] Acharya Atmaramji writes,[5] "The pleasant-feeling-producing karma causes feelings of happiness when we get desirable materials while the unpleasant-feeling-producing karma causes feelings of misery when some undesirable events occur." Thus karma causes only the feelings of happiness and misery; it does not cause gain or loss of material wealth. Jainism does not believe in fate or fortune. The karmas are relevant only to our spiritual states. Acharya Samant Bhadra has written[6]: "If the

---

3 Muni Nemichandra Siddhantidev, in Dravya Sangrah, writes:
SUH-ASUH-BHAAV-JUTTA PUNNAM PAAVAM HAVANTI KHALU JEEVA
SAADAM SUHAU NAAMAM GODAM PUNNAM PARAANI PAAVAM CHA:38:
The souls acquire PUNYA and PAAP on account of auspicious and inauspicious thought-activities, respectively. The pleasant-feeling producing, beneficial life-span-determining, good physique-determining and good status-determining karmas constitute PUNYA, and the rest, PAAP. (The four soul-influencing karmas are certainly PAAP.)

4 Acharya Umaswati's TATTVAARTH SUTRA, Hindi exposition by Pandit Phool Chandra Siddhantacharya, published by Varni Granthmala, Varanasi, India, 1950, pages 382-385.

5 JAIN TATTVA KALIKA (Treatise On Jain Philosophy) by Acharya Atmaramji, published by Atma Gyanpitha, Mansa Mandi, Punjab, 1982, sixth part (KALIKA), page 173.

influx of harmful karma (PAAP) has been stopped, then material wealth is of no consequence, and, if the influx of harmful karma is continuing, then again material wealth is of no avail." Wealth and means of comfort are pseudo-karma (NOKARMA) that are separate from karma. Worldly possessions are acquired by individuals as consequences of their endeavor and suitable opportunity. Some individuals are unhappy in spite of considerable wealth. Some people enjoy happiness though they possess very little material wealth.

Q: How can one survive without indulging in practices which are the norms of contemporary society but may not agree with Jain teachings?

A: There are many honest businessmen and dedicated workers all over the world. At times they win and at times they lose. One can live a life filled with contentment and happiness without indulging in greed and untruth, without compromising the concept of nonviolence. For example, Shrimad Rajchandra, who greatly impressed Mahatma Gandhi, did not compromise his principles in conducting his business.

Q: How can youngsters deal with the problem of 'forced academics'?

A: All parents want their sons and daughters to become professionals in fields like business, law, engineering or medicine. Naturally, parents want the best for their children on account of parental instincts. Youngsters need to understand that all parents have a genuine concern for the welfare of their children. Parents, in turn, need to understand the genuine academic interests of their children. Jainism does not favor one profession over another. All it teaches is that we should do our jobs right, help each other and should not be consumed by money and material.

Q: What does Jainism say about love and marriage?

A: Marriage is a rational intellectual decision. Love is an emotion while physical desire is an instinct. It is imperative that we understand these facts in order to avoid conflicts and minimize mental violence in our lives. Jainism teaches us to avoid situations that may lead to physical or mental violence in interpersonal relationships.

Q: How can we follow the old antiquated traditions regarding marriage in

---

6 YADI PAAP NIRODHONYA SAMPADA KIM PRAYOJANAM
ATHA PAAPAASRAVOSTYANYA SAMPADA KIM PRAYOJANAM:27:
- From RATNAKARAND SHRAAVAKAACHAAR.

modern times? Does Jainism encourage arranged marriages or love marriages?

A: Jainism does not encourage arranged marriages over love marriages or vice versa. As in other aspects of life, regarding marriage as well, we are expected to make rational decisions with the cooperation of all parties involved and take actions based on our belief in nonviolence. Parents should respect the feelings of youngsters and youngsters should understand the concerns of parents for their well-being. There is considerable merit in the input from parents. Dr. Radhakrishnan writes,[7] "It is obvious that since the end of marriage is the enhancement of personality, through the development of mutual relationship based on sex attraction and affection for children, the qualities necessary for making it a success can be judged better by those who are detached, and whose emotions are not already engaged."

Q: What about dating?

A: One of the five vows for householders is partial celibacy which entails refraining from premarital and extramarital intimacy. In other words, friendship is fine but promiscuity is not. It is observed that imprudent conduct may cause serious problems such as AIDS. Further, in general, it leads to serious social problems.

Q: Is divorce advisable in cases where considerable mental violence goes on between husband and wife?

A: Divorce involves tremendous violence and thus it can not be part of the religion of nonviolence. Jainism believes that violence cannot be reduced by violence. It can only be reduced by love and understanding. We should bear in mind that all of us are human and have our shortcomings and weaknesses. So we should try to understand and accommodate each others' views and needs. Further, in divorce, children and other family members suffer unnecessarily.

Q: It is often said that we, the new immigrants, naturally have many problems on account of our attitude and cultural differences. Is that not a fact?

A: Most social problems are not unique to the new immigrants. In general, Jain youngsters have far fewer problems than their American counterparts because of their attitude, family structure and some unique features of their culture. We should preserve

---

7 Religion And Society by Dr. S. Radhakrishnan, published by George Allen and Unwin Ltd, London, fifth impression, 1966, pages 172-173.

these cultural traits. Instinctively, parents look for the welfare of their children. But they should refrain from relentless pursuit of materialism. Youngsters need not compromise the principle of nonviolence under peer pressure. This will help families to avoid numerous problems resulting from the so-called progressive ideas.

Q: This country is said to be the melting pot of various cultures. How can we stay true to our cultural identity?

A: This is a free country where every individual is free to follow his/her own ideas and practice his/her own beliefs. Rather than a melting pot, this country is a mosaic of different cultures. Each culture has its distinct place and plays its unique role for the common good of all without losing its own identity. We Jains can maintain our identity by practicing nonviolence and non-possessiveness. We can make our mark on the society through our professional conduct and business dealings and not through a relentless pursuit of materialism.

Q: What does Jainism say about other religions and philosophies, political and economic systems, and, contemporary customs and practices?

A: Jainism, like Hinduism, teaches us to respect the beliefs held by the followers of other religions. So we Jains do not proselytize. We believe in the freedom of an individual to follow his/her own beliefs and conscience. The Sanskrit word for religion is 'DHARM' meaning duty. Thus, instead of trying to change others, we should fulfill our responsibility towards our children, our parents, our family, our society and humanity at large. This requires sacrifices on our part. It is through such sacrifices that we can collectively achieve our individual freedom. This concept of religion goes far beyond all practices and traditions, ancient or modern, Eastern or Western, legal or expedient. It is beyond all political and economic systems. It is above all theories of psychology and social customs. This is the religion preached by Bhagwaan Mahaveer.

* * * * * * *

People will not judge us by the creed we profess, or the slogans we shout, but by our work, sacrifices, honesty and purity of character. - Mahatma Gandhi

* * * * * * *

## 35 Scriptural View Of The Jain Theory of Karma

Based on Acharya Chandarshi Mahattar's PANCH SANGRAH[1]

While talking about the Jain theory of karma, people commonly make statements such as:

a. Everything is in the hands of God.
b. Jain theory of karma implies 'as you sow, so will you reap'.
c. One has to inevitably experience the fruits of karma.
d. Whatever is destined to happen will happen.
e. Building temples and installing images of 'gods', observing total or partial fasts, organizing worships and celebrations, indulging in charities and visiting places of pilgrimage lead to 'destruction' of karma.
f. Those who are rich and influential have done good deeds such as prayers, worships, donations and religious observances in the past or in their past lives.
g. We should make good 'investment' in our present lives so as to establish beneficial 'credit' for future.

The first statement obviously does not conform to the principles of Jainism. The remaining statements are only partially true. It is worthwhile to elucidate them in the light of Jain scriptures.

The Sanskrit word 'karma' literally means actions or deeds. Gita, one of the most sacred books of Hinduism, says:

KARMANYEVAADHIKAARASTE MA PHALESHU KADAACHAN
MA KARMAPHAL-HETURBHUR MA TE SANGOSTVAKARMANI:2-47:

"Action (effort) alone is thy province, never the fruits thereof[2]; let not thy motive be the fruits of action, nor shouldst thou desire to avoid action."[3]

---

1 Hindi exposition of Acharya Chandarshi Mahattar's PANCH SANGRAH (9-10 century A.D.) by Marudhar Kesari Shri Mishrimalji Maharaj, edited by Dev Kumar Jain, published by Acharya Shri Raghunath Jain Research Institute, Jodhpur, Rajasthan, India, 1985-86.

2 According to the Jain theory of karma, at times, pseudo-karmas (NOKARMA, also called NIMITTA) such as our circumstances and events beyond our control might influence the course of our lives.

3 The Gita According To Gandhi, translated from Gujarati into English by Mahadev Desai, Navajivan Publishing House, Ahmedabad, India, 1984, page 161.

This statement agrees, for most part, with the Jain theory of karma, though, in Jainism, karmas do not mean actions or deeds. Jain philosophy says that karmas are extremely fine particles of matter that become associated with the worldly souls on account of their feelings and emotions. Further, according to Jainism, the fruition of karma can be modified or changed as explained below.

**What is karma?**

Worldly souls, on account of attachment and aversion (RAAG and DWESH), continuously undergo pulsations. Because of these pulsations, the soul attracts ultra fine particles of matter which become associated with the soul. These particles are called material karmas (DRAVYA KARMA). Another kind of karmas are abstract karmas (BHAAV KARMA), which include attachment and aversion; passions of anger, pride, deceit and greed; and, the combined activities of body, speech and mind (YOGA). These cause the influx and bonding of material karmas. Essentially, irrationalism (MITHYAATVA), non-restraint (AVIRATI), carelessness (PRAMAAD), passions (KASHAAYA) and activities of body, speech and mind (YOGA) are responsible for karmic bondage.[4] It should be noted that karmas influence our thoughts and feelings. Thus karmas might lead to feelings of happiness or unhappiness in a worldly soul. Karmas have little to do with materials such as wealth and other means of creature comfort.

Good thoughts and feelings such as compassion, brotherhood and goodwill cause the influx of meritorious (PUNYA) karmas while thoughts and feelings of anger, pride, ego, desire for name and fame, greed and deceit cause the influx of demeritorious (PAAP) karmas. One should bear in mind that, in the ultimate analysis, all karmas are undesirable.

There are four aspects of karmic bondage with a worldly soul:

1. Nature or kind

   There are eight kinds of karmas:
   Knowledge-obscuring (JNAANA VARNI)
   Perception-obscuring (DARSHANA VARNI)
   Feeling-producing (VEDANEEYA)
   Deluding (MOHANEEYA)
   Life-span determining (AYU)
   Physique-determining (NAAM)
   Status-determining (GOTRA)

---

4 PANCH SANGRAH, volume 6, page 14.

Obstructing (ANTARAAYA)

Knowledge-obscuring, perception-obscuring, deluding and obstructing karmas directly influence the soul. So they are called soul-influencing (GHATEEYA) karmas. The remaining karmas influence the physical being of a worldly soul and are called AGHATEEYA karmas.

2. Quantity of karma particles (PRADESH)
3. Duration for which the karma particles will remain associated with the soul (STHITI)
4. Intensity of fruition (ANUBHAAG).

The nature and intensity of physical and mental activities (thoughts and feelings) of a living being determine (establish) the type and quantity of karma particles which become associated with the worldly soul. The intensity of passions determines the duration of association of the karmas and the severity (gravity) of fruition (consequences) of karmas. In general, a group of karma particles remains quiescent (dormant) for a certain time interval, then it becomes operative. During fruition, karmas may influence the thoughts and feelings of the worldly being. Upon fruition, the karma particles are shed by the soul.

**Some questions addressed by the Jain theory of karma**[5]

The Jain theory of karma is quite intricate and sophisticated. It addresses the following important questions among others:

In view of the Jain theory of karma, is everything predestined? Or:

a. Can the moment of fruition of karma be altered? If yes, then what kind of thoughts and feelings are necessary for the purpose?
b. Can one type of karma be converted into another kind? Can demeritorious karma be transformed into meritorious karma and vice versa?
c. Can the severity of fruition of karma be reduced or increased?
d. Can the fruition of a powerful karma be prevented? If yes, how?

**Transformations of karma**

In PANCH SANGRAH, Acharya Chandarshi Mahattar has answered these questions and has presented a detailed and elaborate account of the transformations of karma. Other Jain scriptures contain almost identical concepts.

A brief account of some states and transformations of karma is presented below.[6]

5 PANCH SANGRAH, volume 6, page 13.

6 PANCH SANGRAH, volume 6, page 16. Volumes 6, 7 and 8 of PANCH

Operation (UDAYA): The state of karma during fruition (producing feelings of happiness and unhappiness) is called operation. At the end of the state of operation, the karma particles are shed by the soul.

Premature Operation (UDEERANA): When certain karma particles are made to become operative before their predetermined time, it is called premature operation. Just as fruits can be ripened before time by careful processing, similarly, through proper thoughts and effort, the consequences of karma particles can be endured prematurely.

Generally, when a given type of karma is operative, similar type of karma particles (which, at the time of bonding, were established to be operative in the future) can be made to become operative prematurely.

Augmentation (UDVARTANA or UTKARSHAN): The duration and intensity of fruition of karma particles are determined by the intensity of passions at the time of bonding. Subsequent increase in duration and intensity that may occur because of thoughts and endeavor is called augmentation.

Diminution (APVARTANA or APKARSHAN): This is the opposite of augmentation. The decrease in duration and intensity of karma particles that may occur because of thoughts and endeavor is called diminution.

Mutation (SANKRAMAN): The conversion of one type of karma particles into another type of karma is called mutation of karma.

Mutation takes place between the subtypes of a given type of karma. Mutation does not occur between karma particles of different types.[7] There are certain exceptions to the mutation of karma particles belonging to the same type. For example, no mutation occurs between the four subtypes of life-span-determining karma. Further, perception-deluding karma can not be converted into conduct-deluding karma and vice versa.

Subsidence (UPASHAMAN): The state of karma in which operation or

SANGRAH contain a detailed discussion of these transformations.

7 For example, unpleasant-feeling-producing karma can be converted into pleasant-feeling-producing karma and vice versa because unpleasant-feeling-producing and pleasant-feeling-producing karma are subtypes of the same type of (feeling-producing) karma. High status-determining karma can not be converted into pleasant- (or unpleasant-) feeling-producing karma. - D. C. J.

premature operation of karma does not occur is called subsidence. In such a state, augmentation, diminution and mutation are possible. As soon as the duration of subsidence of a particular group of karma particles is over, those karma particles become operative and are shed upon fruition.

Prevention (NIDHATTI): This is the state of karma particles in which premature operation and mutation are not possible. Augmentation and diminution, however, do occur in the state of prevention.

Invariance (NIKAACHANA): This is the state of karma particles in which premature operation, mutation, augmentation and diminution do not take place. In this state, the fruition of karma particles can not be modified or altered. Their consequences are the same as were established at the time of bonding. A few subtypes of karmas fall into this category without exception.

A worldly soul continuously acquires new karma particles. Nevertheless, at any instant, the mode of bonding of all karmas is not identical. Nature, quantity, duration and intensity of various karmas which become associated with the soul at any given moment are different. Moreover, a given set of karma particles does not necessarily produce the same consequences as were established at the time of bonding. On fruition, some karma particles may influence the thoughts and feelings of a living being the same way as demarcated at the time of bonding. Other karma particles may cause thoughts and feelings that are different from those established at the time of bonding. Certain karma particles come to fruition earlier or later, for shorter or longer duration, with milder or greater intensity, while other karma particles are shed by the living being without fruition.[8]

It is obvious that abstract (BHAAV) karmas (our thoughts and feelings) play an extremely important role in bonding and operation of karmas. There are fourteen stages of spiritual development based on the purity of thoughts and feelings of a living being.[9] The transformations of karmas described above are closely related to these stages of spiritual development.

## Some implications of the Jain theory of karma

The above concepts indicate that the life of an individual is regulated by the interactions between his soul and matter (karma particles and the environment). Thus there are many significant

8 PANCH SANGRAH, volume 6, page 18.

9 Lesson 19

implications of the Jain theory of karma in our daily lives. The Jain theory of karma encompasses our individual lives, our family life and our social life. Our thoughts and actions as individuals, as members of our community and as citizens of the world should be guided by our concepts of the Jain theory of karma.

The influx, bonding and operation of karmas is a continuous process. Therefore, it is necessary for us to have good thoughts and feelings at all times; not just when we are in a temple or at a religious celebration. While indulging in any worldly affair or even performing a religious activity, we accumulate undesirable karma by having passions such as anger, pride, intrigue and greed, by having fear or anxiety, by having desires or ulterior motives, by having our eyes set on material goals or by seeking social status and fame. For example, a doctor, scientist, industrialist, businessman or engineer having the goal of obtaining material possessions and means of comfort will obtain considerable demeritorious karma. On the other hand, an individual, performing the same duties with a view to fulfilling his/her responsibility towards others, obtains mild and meritorious karma. A person, making charitable contributions or performing penance of various kinds with the intention of satisfying his/her ego by gaining recognition and fame, obviously has passions and thus he/she accumulates mostly demeritorious karma (PAAP). Further, the more intense the desire, the more durable and acute the demeritorious karma that are obtained. Even the desire for better life in the present or in the future is detrimental to spiritual progress.

Since the influx, bonding, transformations and fruition of karma depend on our thoughts and feelings, mere physical activities are not sufficient for spiritual progress. A religious activity such as prayer, worship or fasting performed without proper thoughts and understanding has no real significance. The true practice of religion consists in having good feelings and pure thoughts. Jainism teaches that conduct without rational perception and rational knowledge is not rational or proper.

## Charity: A Jain Scriptural View

by Dr. Trilok Chandra Jain Shastri

All religions extol the virtue of charity or donation. Everybody agrees that helping others by donating money and material is admirable. Many individuals, from the venerable monks and scholars to the poor and sick, depend on the generosity of society. Religious institutions run on donations.

### What Is Charity?

The Sanskrit word for charity or donation is DAAN, which literally means giving. In TATTVAARTH SUTRA, Acharya Umaswati has defined:

अनुग्रहार्थं स्वस्यातिसर्गो दानम् । 7-38 ।

ANUGRAHAARTHAM SWASYAATISARGO DAANAM

Charity entails giving one's wealth for mutual benefits.

In this aphorism, the phrase 'mutual benefit' is important. The donor does not give only for the benefit of the recipient. He/she performs charity for the benefit of the self. This implies that the donor does not have any feelings of superiority or ego or desire for recognition. The donor does not think that he/she is doing a favor.

The prime recipients of charity are monks and religious institutions. The monks follow the path to spiritual advancement. They have no passions for enhancing their position. They have equanimity and peace of mind. Thus they exemplify the path to achieving true happiness and harmony in life. In return, the householders provide means of subsistence for them. Religious institutions, including temples, places of pilgrimage and educational institutions, provide us with an opportunity to learn the teachings of our religion. They epitomize virtues such as nonviolence, truth and non-possessiveness. So we support them. Some people, in spite of their sincere efforts to be self-sufficient, do not have the necessary means of subsistence because of circumstances beyond their control. So they deserve our help.

### Four Kinds of Charity

According to Jainism, charity is of four kinds: donation of medicine

(AUSHADHI), donation of books (SHAASTRA), donation of food (AHAAR) and delivering freedom from fear (ABHAYA). These four kinds of donations are meant to fulfill the needs of the body, mind and soul of the recipient. Food and medicines are essential for the growth and maintenance of body. They are needed for sustenance of life. Jain monks do not indulge in worldly activities such as earning livelihood, cooking and shopping. The householders provide them with food and shelter. The monks accept these materials from the householders according to the rules set in the scriptures. Providing books and other means for enhancing their knowledge of the scriptures to monks as well as to householders constitutes the gift of knowledge. Householders need to have a proper education for earning their livelihood and become productive members of society. Thus supporting schools, colleges and universities is also a gift of knowledge.

Delivering protection and freedom from fear is essential for the well-being of men and women. This concept is extended to all living beings. It not only implies ensuring that we do not deliberately hurt or kill any form of life, but it also entails conservation of natural resources and protection of the environment. Further, to effect freedom from fear and suspicion, it is essential to establish an atmosphere of understanding and trust among men and women. As mentioned earlier, charity is for the mutual welfare of all. Therefore, this kind of charity is most august.

Describing the unique features of charity, Acharya Umaswati says:

विधिद्रव्यदातृपात्रविशेषात्तद्विशेषः ।7-39 ।

VIDHIDRAVYADAATRIPAATRAVISHESHAATTADVISHESHAH

Charity is distinguished by procedure, material, donor and recipient.

### Qualities of a Donor

In PURUSHAARTH SIDDHYUPAAYA, Acharya Amrit Chandra Suri has described the qualities of a donor as follows:[1]

1. A donor has no desire for reward or compensation of any kind such as fame and fortune, profit and prosperity.
2. A donor maintains composure if things do not go as planned.
3. A donor is sincere. He does not indulge in complicity to

---

1 ऐहिकफलानुपेक्षा क्षान्तिर्निष्कपटतानसूयत्वम् ।
अविषादित्वमुदित्वे निरहङ्कारित्वमिति हि दातृगुणाः ।169 ।

circumvent the rules established by society and government.

4. A donor refrains from envy and competition.
5. A donor has no feelings of remorse or guilt. Once the donation is made, he/she is totally unconcerned about its quality and value.
6. A donor does not have the feelings of exhilaration. A donor is modest. He/she understands that the material being donated does not belong exclusively to him/her. Thus he/she considers himself/herself as merely an instrument (NIMITTA) in the process of giving.
7. A donor is free from ego.

Acharya Siddhasen, in his commentary on TATTVAARTH SUTRA, recounts the following qualities of a donor:[2]

a. Absence of ill-will towards the recipient (ANUSOOYATVA)
b. Absence of dejection in giving (AVISHAADITVA)
c. Absence of condescension towards the recipient (NIRAHAN-KAARITVA). This means that the donor does not consider himself/herself to be superior to the recipient.
d. Joy in giving (MUDITVA). This implies absence of remorse or guilt.
e. Auspicious frame of mind (forbearance, KSHAMA)
f. Absence of desire for material gains (AIHIKPHALANAPEKSHA)
g. Absence of complicity (NISHKAPATA)
h. Absence of craving for rebirth in a desirable form (ANIDAANATVA)

It should be noted that the qualities of a donor enumerated by Acharya Amrit Chandra Suri are essentially the same as those described by Acharya Siddhasen. *Evidently, we Jains and our system have a lot to learn from our scriptures.*

### Material Appropriate for Donation

Describing the materials suitable for donation, Acharya Amrit Chandra Suri has written, in PURUSHAARTH SIDDHYUPAAYA:[3] Things that generate attachment, aversion, incontinence (lack of self-control), vanity, pain and fright should not be donated. Only such

2 Jaina Yoga by R. Williams, published by Motilal Banarsidass, Delhi, 1983, page 153.

3 रागद्वेषासंयममददुःखभयादिकं न यत्कुरुते ।
द्रव्यं तदेव देयं सुतपः स्वाध्याय वृद्धिकरम् ।170 ।

things that promote self-study and observance of austerities should be donated. In other words, one should not donate means of material comforts, unhealthy foods, and dangerous items such as knives, guns and poison. One should donate Items that promote good physical and mental health such as nourishing foods, medicine and books.

## Qualities of a Recipient

Jain scriptures emphasize that donation should be given to the four segments of the Jain order (SANGH): monks, nuns, laymen and laywomen. Qualities of a recipient have also been defined by Acharya Amrit Chandra Suri, in PURUSHAARTH SIDDHYUPAAYA, in the following words:[4] The recipients belong to three classes depending upon the level of their rationalism, which eventually leads to salvation: those who possess rational perception but do not practice any vows, householders who practice the minor vows, and monks who practice the major vows.

Does this mean that we should help only those who belong to the Jain community? Well, Jainism can not condone discrimination on the basis of religion or creed. We should help all regardless of their religious beliefs. By saying that the recipient should have rational perception, Acharya Amrit Chandra Suri implies that we should not support individuals who spread irrationalism, delusions and superstition, and who mislead their unsuspecting followers to fulfill their ulterior designs. We should not help unscrupulous and anti-social elements including institutions that indulge in circumventing the teachings of religion and government regulations. We should help individuals who are spiritually advanced. Individuals who have rational perception refrain from spreading irrationalism and delusion. They do not exploit the masses for achieving name and fame, recognition and titles. They have no material goals and lead a virtuous life. They enjoy contentment and equanimity. Thus they epitomize the path to real happiness. Ordinary people who lead a clean and virtuous life also deserve our support.

## Procedure of Donation

The procedure of donation has been described in considerable detail in the Jain scriptures. Most of the discussion centers on the ways food

---

4 पात्रं त्रिभेदमुक्तं संयोगो मोक्षकारण गुणानाम् ।
अविरतसम्यग्दृष्टिः विरताविरतश्च सकलविरतश्च ।171 ।

is offered to the monks and nuns. Commenting on the procedure of donation, Pandit Phool Chandra Jain Siddhantacharya writes:[5] The donor accords reception, seat, washing the feet, worship (praise) and respectful gestures (bowing) appropriate to the recipient. The donor makes the donation with purity of mind, speech and body. He/she offers food and other materials beneficial to the recipient. The appropriate reception, seating, respectful gestures and materials such as food, water and books are determined according to time and place, and considering the nature and capability of the recipient.

## Concluding Remarks

The Jain religion teaches that our thoughts, speech and actions should be rational. However, many times some individuals and institutions exploit the sentiments of credulous people and procure donations to fulfill their own interests and ambitions. Sometimes, donations are used improperly. A variety of schemes are employed in collecting donations. All this goes on in the name of religion. In the light of the teachings of our scriptures, we Jains should not indulge in such practices.

* * * * * * *

. . . the economic factor is an essential element in human life. There is no sin in wealth, just as there is no virtue in poverty. The efforts of anyone to increase his wealth cannot be condemned, but if the pursuit of wealth means loss to others, monetary or moral, then the question arises whether the acquisition of wealth by such methods and with such results is right. The Hindu code insists on the motive of social service, not personal gain.

Dr. S. Radhakrishnan

* * * * * * *

---

5 TATTVAARTH SUTRA, Hindi exposition by Pandit Phool Chandra Jain Siddhantacharya, published by Varni Granthmala, Varanasi, 1950, page 365.

## Jain Scriptures

by Chandrakant P. Shah, Pravin K. Shah and Duli Chandra Jain

DCJ: What are Jain scriptures and who composed them?

CPS: Jains believe that TEERTHANKARs are omniscient (KEVALI). They know the absolute truth about reality (VASTU SWAROOP). TEERTHANKAR Mahaveer imparted the knowledge of reality to his GANADHARs (interpreters), Gautam Swami being the chief among them. Gautam Swami and other GANADHARs then composed the Jain scriptures. Later, the scriptural knowledge was passed on by word of mouth from one generation of acharyas to the next. These acharyas were called SHRUT KEVALIs meaning the scholars of scriptures.[1] They had excellent memory and were chosen to study and memorize the scriptures.

DCJ: Under such conditions, there is some chance of variation in the text and interpretation of the scriptures. Is that true?

PKS: Yes. Gradually, some differences in words and phrases, verses and aphorisms came about. Some acharyas noticed that the scriptures were gradually being forgotten. So a number of councils were organized to restore the scriptures and transcribe them.

DCJ: In ancient times, the scriptures were written on palm-leaves (TAADAPATRAs). How durable were they?

PKS: The leaves did not last for many years. Even these days, books do not last long. Some portions of the scriptures would disintegrate. Some words would fade away. Thus they were copied over again. The acharyas who wrote expositions and commentaries on the original scriptures were required to guess some words, phrases and verses. It should be noted that the Jain scriptures have gone through the same kind of processes as scriptures of other religions in the history of mankind.

CPS: In view of the above, what should we Jains believe in?

DCJ: Jains believe that the knowledge attained by an omniscient KEVALI is the absolute truth. In the light of the principle of relativism

1 The Sanskrit word SHRUT means what is heard or the knowledge derived through words. Hence the word SHRUT is used for our scriptures.

(SYAADAVAAD), we believe that those who are not omniscient can know only relative truth. We can not attain the absolute knowledge of reality without becoming omniscients. The theory of multiplicity of viewpoints (ANEKAANTAVAAD) maintains that the concept of reality formed by a person based on his/her observation and experience is appropriate from his/her point of view. Further, an individual's concept of reality changes with his/her observations and experiences. These changes occur on account of evolution in personality (DRAVYA), environment (KSHETRA), time (KAAL) and experience (BHAAV). We do not believe in the infallibility of any book or teacher. That is why Jains were called NIRGRANTHs (those without any tome).

PKS: This implies that my concept of religion might be different from your concept of religion. How can we both be correct?

DCJ: Our concepts of religion are correct from our respective viewpoints. The only condition is that our concepts should not compromise our beliefs in rationalism and nonviolence. The Jain belief in the concept of nonviolence is infallible.

CPS: If it is so, why are Jains divided into Digambars, Shwetambars, Sthanakvasis, Taranpanthis?

PKS: First, the doctrine accepted by all Jains is one and the same. Thus Digambar, Shwetambar, Sthanakvasi, etc., are not sects of Jainism. These divisions occurred because of differences of opinion regarding the scriptural knowledge and religious practices. Such differences could have been resolved in view of our belief in the doctrine of multiplicity of viewpoints. However, geographic separations, differences in languages and human weaknesses played their role in fragmenting the Jain society. For example, those who lived in one part of the country, called Jain scriptures AGAMs while others called them SHASTRAs although the words AGAM and SHASTRA have the same meaning. Some people preferred to use the language ARDHA MAAGADHI for their scriptures while others used PRAKRIT or Sanskrit for their scriptures. Some individuals became too zealous about protecting and propagating their own views in order to maintain a tight control over their followers. This process led to the divisions that we see today. It is distressing that this process is still going on in our community.

DCJ: We believe that Bhagwaan Mahaveer's interpreters (GANADHARs) systematically organized the scriptural knowledge of the Jain religion and composed the Jain scriptures. Will you please describe the classification of the Jain scriptures?

PKS: Traditionally, the scriptures composed by the interpreters are classified into two broad categories: The main volumes (12 ANGAs) and the prior volumes (14 PURVAs).[2] The Sanskrit names of the twelve main volumes and their contents are:

1. ACHAARAANG describes the conduct of a monk and the penance of Mahaveer. Its language indicates that it is the oldest scripture.
2. SUTRA-KRITAANG describes the principle of nonviolence and the Jain concept of the universe. It also contains the refutation of certain other schools of thought.
3. STHAANAANG consists of the discussion of the basic substances of the universe such as living beings (JEEVs) in a schematic manner.
4. SAMAVAAYAANG provides the comprehensive knowledge of the universal constituents and concepts in the light of substance (DRAVYA), environment (KSHETRA), time (KAAL) and experience (BHAAV)[3].
5. VYAAKHYA-PRAJNYAPTI is the largest of the main volumes and contains 36,000 questions and answers about soul, matter, etc. It is also called BHAGWATI SUTRA.[4] It should be noted that in BHAGWATI SUTRA, Bhagwaan Mahaveer responds to each question with the statement "subject to qualification" in view of the Jain principle of relativism (SYAADAVAAD).
6. JNAATRI-DHARMA-KATHA contains stories illustrating the principles and teachings of the Jain religion.
7. UPAASAKA-DHYAYANAANG describes the code of conduct of Jain householders (SHRAAVAKs) and contains the stories of ten householders who religiously followed Bhagwaan Mahaveer's teachings.

---

2 Some scholars believe that later the prior volumes (PURVAs) were incorporated in the twelfth main volume (ANGA).

3 TEERTHANKAR MAHAVEER AUR UNKI ACHARYA PARAMPARA by Dr. Nemi Chandra Shastri Jyotishacharya, published by Digambar Jain Vidvat Parishad, volume 2, page 11.

4 The Jaina Path Of Purification by Padmanabh S. Jaini, published by Motilal Banarsidass, Delhi, 1979, page 318.

8. ANTAH-KRIT-DASHAANG contains the stories of ten monks who became omniscient and attained salvation by destroying their karma.
9. ANUTTAROPAPAADIK describes the life of ten monks who attained the status of heavenly beings called ANUTTAR.
10. PRASHNA-VYAAKARANAANG contains questions, answers and stories regarding the five major vows (MAHAVRATs) and demerit (PAAP).
11. VIPAAKA-SUTRAANG explains the consequences of good and bad karma through several stories.
12. DRISHTI-VAADAANG consists of five segments. Its most important segment constitutes the prior volumes (14 PURVAs)[5]. It is believed that these fourteen volumes are of great antiquity going back to the time of Bhagwaan Parshvanath. For this reason, these are called the prior volumes. Bhagwaan Mahaveer's interpreters reorganized this valuable knowledge and incorporated much of it in the main volumes (ANGAs).[6]

CPS: Do all Jains accept the twelve main volumes (ANGAs) and the fourteen prior volumes (PURVAs)?

DCJ: Yes, all Jains, Digambars as well as Shwetambars, agree that Bhagwaan Mahaveer's interpreters composed the twelve main volumes and the fourteen prior volumes.

PKS: It is seen that the subject matter of the above mentioned scriptures overlaps. Is there any other classification of these scriptures?

CPS: All Jain scriptures, including the latter ones, have been classified into the following four categories depending upon their contents:[7]

---

5 The Sanskrit names of the fourteen prior volumes are: UTPAADA-PURVA, AGRAAYANIYA, VEERYAANU-PRAVAAD, ASTINAASTI-PRAVAAD, JNAANA-PRAVAAD, SATYA-PRAVAAD, ATMA-PRAVAAD, KARMA-PRAVAAD, PRATYAAKHYAAN-NAAMDHEYA, VIDYAANU-VAAD, KALYAAN-NAAMDHEYA, PRAANAAVAAYA, KRIYA-VISHAAL, LOKABINDU-SAAR.

6 The Jaina Path Of Purification, page 49.

7 Agam Anuyog Trust (Sthanakvasi Society), Ahmedabad, India is publishing the thirty-two scriptures (AGAMS) classified in these categories under the direction of Pandit Dalsukhbhai Malvania. It does call the fourth category KARANA-ANUYOGA as GANITA-ANUYOGA (mathematical expositions).

I. Primary expositions (PRATHAMA-ANUYOGA) consist of life stories of important religious personalities and moral stories.

II. The expositions of aspects of reality (DRAVYA-ANUYOGA) contain discussions of soul, karma, the principle of multiplicity of viewpoints and the like.

III. The expositions of ethical code (CHARANA-ANUYOGA) describe the code of conduct of monks, nuns and householders.

IV. The expositions of physical universe (KARANA-ANUYOGA) contain such sciences as ancient cosmology and astronomy.

DCJ: Are all these original scriptures available today?

PKS: As mentioned above, in the beginning, the scriptures were memorized by scholarly monks (SHRUT KEVALIs). The original scriptures were preserved orally for about 150 years. Approximately 170 years after Bhagwaan Mahaveer's NIRVANA, during the reign of Emperor Chandra Gupta Maurya, a severe famine occurred in North India for twelve years. Acharya Bhadrabahu Swami was the head of the Jain order (SANGH). He was recognized by all Jains, Digambars as well as Shwetambars. Bhadrabahu realized that during those hard times it would be very difficult for the Jain monks to follow their code of conduct (such as daily recitation and study of scriptures, etc.). Therefore, along with his twelve thousand disciples, he traveled south where they could follow the strict code of conduct for monks. However, a number of monks stayed north. They were led by Acharya Sthulabhadra who relaxed some of the rules so that they could survive during the famine.

DCJ: How was the scriptural knowledge affected by these events?

CPS: The last person to know all fourteen prior volumes (PURVAs) (and all twelve main volumes, ANGAs) was Acharya Bhadrabahu (3rd century B.C.). During the famine, portions of fourteen prior texts were forgotten. In fact, Jainism passed through a crisis. Acharya Sthulabhadra realized that much of the scriptural knowledge would be lost if steps were not taken to restore the scriptures. So he organized a council of Jain scholars at Patliputra (Patna in Bihar) to consolidate the remaining knowledge and to restore the scriptural texts. Acharya Bhadrabahu was on his way to Nepal and did not come to Patliputra. However, he did send his representative monks who were scholars of the first eleven main volumes (ANGAs) to the council. Although, the twelfth main volume (DRISHTIVAADAANG) including the fourteen prior volumes (PURVAs) were lost in their original form, portions of their contents exist even today in other scriptures. The original ANGAs as well as subsidiary (ANGABAAHYA) scriptures were put in written form sometime after the Patliputra Council. A second council was held at Mathura in the fourth century A.D. under the guidance of Acharya Skandila. Another council was held concurrently at Valabhi under the supervision of Acharya Nagarajuna. Obviously, there were some differences between the versions of the scriptures prepared at the two councils. These differences were reconciled at the third and last council held at Valabhi that took place about 980 years after Bhagwaan Mahaveer's NIRVANA. At that council, Acharya Devaardhigani Kshamaashraman compiled the final revised versions of the existing scriptures and had them committed to writing in their entirety.[8]

PKS: Do all Jains consider these scriptures to be the "original" ones composed by Bhagwaan Mahaveer's interpreters?

CPS: It is evident from the above discussion that the Jain scriptures recompiled by Devaardhigani Kshamaashraman are as close to the original ones as one can expect under the circumstances. The Digambar Jains do not accept them as "original" while the Shwetambar jains do. However, both groups agree that the scriptures have gone through many revisions and portions of them have been lost. In view of this fact, all Jains should study the scriptures belonging to both the Digambar and Shwetambar traditions.

DCJ: Is this the complete story of the Jain scriptures?

PKS: In addition to the scriptures composed by the interpreters, there are many scriptures composed by various acharyas and scholars. These are called subsidiary (ANGABAAHYA) scriptures. The subsidiary scriptures are divided into five categories: Secondary volumes (12 UPAANGs), disciplinary volumes (6 CHEDA-SUTRAs), basic volumes (4 MOOL-SUTRAs), miscellaneous volumes (10 PRAKEERNAKA-SUTRAs) and supplementary volumes (2 CHOOLIKA-SUTRAs). Thus there are 34 subsidiary scriptures. Some well-known subsidiary scriptures are:

8 The Jaina Path Of Purification, page 52.

(a) DASHA-SHRUT-SKANDH-SUTRA which contains ten chapters. One of the ten chapters of this scripture is KALPASUTRA which is recited during the celebration of spiritual awareness (PARYUSHAN).

(b) AVASHYAK-SUTRA which describes the six essential daily practices, namely, equanimity (SAAMAAYIK), worship of TEERTHANKARs (CHATURVINSHATI STAV), reverence (VANDANA), introspection (PRATIKRAMAN), renunciation of body (KAAYOTSARG) and resolution (PRATYAAKHYAAN).

(c) DASHAVAIKAALIK SUTRA composed by Arya Shayyambhav (around 429 B.C.) describes the conduct of monks.

(d) UTTARAADHYAYAN SUTRA contains teachings of Jain religion. It also has stories and dialogues about the Jain teachings.

CPS: What are some of the oldest Jain scriptures according to modern scholars?

DCJ: There is some difference of opinion on this point among the various scholars. Dr. Bool Chand Jain writes[9]: Jacobi is of the opinion that the first book (SHRUT SKANDH) of the ACHAARAANG-SUTRA and the SUTRAKRATANG-SUTRA may be reckoned among the most ancient parts of the Jain scriptures. The date of these SUTRAs would be the fourth century B.C. The second book of ACHAARAANG which obviously is a later composition and which does not even fit in with the scheme of writing adopted in the first book, refers possibly, in point of time, to the first part of the third century B.C. when the whole canon was brought under the patriarchate of Sthulabhadra. According to K. C. Lalwani, DASHAVAIKAALIK SUTRA was composed around 429 B.C.[10] Thus it could be one of the oldest scriptures.

CPS: What are the beliefs in the Digambar tradition about the scriptures?

DCJ: The Digambar Jains accept fourteen subsidiary scriptures. These include DASHAVAIKAALIK SUTRA and UTTARAADHYAYAN SUTRA.[11] According to Digambar sources, when the original 12

9 Lord Mahavira by Dr. Bool Chand Jain, published by Jain Cultural Research Society, Parshvanath Vidyashram, Banaras, 1948.

10 Arya Shayyambhava's DASAVAIKALIKA SUTRA, translated by Kastur Chand Lalwani, Motilal Banarsidass, Delhi, 1973, page vi.

11 TEERTHANKAR MAHAVEER AUR UNKI ACHARYA PARAMPARA by Dr. Nemi Chandra Shastri Jyotishacharya, published by Digambar Jain

main scriptures and 14 prior scriptures were forgotten, acharyas composed scriptures based on the existing knowledge of the principles of Jainism. Acharya Gunadhar (about 1st century A.D.) composed KASAAYAPAAHUD. It has 233 couplets, each couplet being an aphorism. It presents the theory of karma in relation to the binding of deluding karma. Acharya Veersen and Acharya Jinasen II (about 8th century A.D.) composed its exposition (JAYADHAVALA TIKA). Acharya Veersen wrote about a third of the exposition (equivalent to about 20,000 couplets) and Acharya Jinasen wrote the remaining portion. It has been published in 15 volumes. Another extensive work on the theory of karma is SHATKHANDAAGAM composed by Acharya Pushpadant and Acharya Bhootabali who were the disciples of Acharya Dharsen (about 1st century A.D.). It consists of six sections: JEEVATTHAN, KHUDDA BANDH, BANDH SAAMITTA VICHAYA, VEYANA, VAGGANA and MAHABANDH. Acharya Veersen has composed its exposition (DHAVALA TIKA) which is equivalent to 72,000 couplets. The first five sections of SHATKHANDAAGAM have been published in 16 volumes while the last section MAHABANDH has been published in 7 volumes.

PKS: What about the works of some other acharyas?

CPS: Acharya Kundkund (about 2nd century A.D.) composed eight PAAHUD texts on perception, knowledge, conduct, liberation, etc. He also wrote PANCHASTIKAYA-SAAR (describing the six entities that comprise the universe), SAMAYA-SAAR (containing the basic concepts regarding soul and other entities) and NIYAM-SAAR (providing the code of conduct). Written in 2nd century A. D., MOOLAACHAAR of Acharya Vattker is an important work containing the essence of ACHAARAANG SUTRA. Acharya Nemi Chandra Siddhanta Chakravarti (about tenth century A.D.) wrote GOMMATSAAR JEEVAKAAND and KARMAKAAND that contain the Jain concepts of soul and the theory of karma. These are based on the scriptures SHATKHANDAAGAM.

DCJ: Are there any scriptures which are recognized as authentic in both Digambar and Shwetambar traditions?

CPS: Acharya Umaswati (about 2nd century A.D.) wrote TATTVAARTH SUTRA. It is a systematic and comprehensive presentation of the

---

Vidvat Parishad, volume 2, page 14.

principles of Jainism. It describes the seven aspects of reality, the theory of karma and the path to liberation. Acharya Siddhasen Divakar (5th century A.D.) wrote NYAAYAAVATAAR and SANMATITARK, the two important works on Jain logic. All Jains accept these scriptures.

PKS: We have presented a brief description of the Jain scriptures. It shows that the Jain literature is quite extensive. In some cases, scholars have disagreement regarding the chronology and names of authors of certain texts. Some minor variations in the facts and interpretation are natural. In spite of this, all scholars agree that the doctrine of Jainism exhibits a remarkable unity. Dr. Padmanabh Jaini, in Jaina Path Of Purification, writes that the two Jain groups have exhibited "their remarkable unwillingness to depart from their basic doctrines and practices". He writes, "As for arguments between acharyas over minor philosophical issues, these have traditionally been accommodated with the spirit of SYAADVAAD (doctrine of relativism)." He continues, "The basic Jaina doctrines thus show an extraordinary uniformity through the centuries; indeed it is possible to consider them as a coherent whole." In sum, it can be said that all scriptures belonging to Digambar as well as Shwetambar traditions, present the same Jain doctrines.

* * * * * * *

. . . in this poison tree of SAMSAAR (worldly existence) are two fruits of incomparable value. They are the enjoyment of great books and the company of good souls. If we want to absorb the fruits of great literature, we must read them not as we do cricket stories but read them with concentration.

- Dr. S. Radhakrishnan

* * * * * * *

# The Doctrine Of Relativism

by Shri T. U. Mehta[1]

"Of ten things that annoy us, nine would not be able to do so, if we understood them thoroughly in their own causes, and therefore, know their necessity and true nature. . . . To see things purely as objects of understanding is to rise to freedom." - Schopenhauer

A proper understanding of conflicting factors in individual or social life is like the oiling of a global mechanism. It smooths relations between individuals, societies and nations. How to arrive at such an understanding? The doctrine of relativism (SYAADAVAAD) which is also known as the principle of multiplicity of viewpoints (ANEKAANTAVAAD) presents a technique for understanding and analyzing each premise or situation. The basic theory is that truth is revealed to us only partially when we look at a thing from a single aspect. Suppose we find a proposition which is contrary to what we believe to be a fact and so we have grave reservations about it. If we apply the principle of multiplicity of viewpoints and analyze it from other points of view, we will be able to understand the cause of our disagreement and there is a good chance that our concerns about it will be alleviated.

## Why Relativism?

When we make a judgement about an object, that judgement is based, among other things, not only on the intrinsic nature of that object (DRAVYA) but also on the place (KSHETRA), the time (KAAL) and our concept or attitude (BHAAV). The last one can be our viewpoint. Our impression depends much upon our subjective judgement and our recollection of the past experiences about similar objects. Our prejudices and predilections, our social upbringing, our environmental needs, and our political and social preferences also play a very decisive role, especially when we are making a judgement about an idea. Thus it is extremely important to analyze every object and every idea, which have infinite characteristics, from a variety of standpoints.

The doctrine of relativism is based on the following facts:

1. Everything in the universe has infinite characteristics.
2. A human being with his/her limited capabilities cannot

1 Adapted from 'The Path of Arhat: A Religious Democracy' by T. U. Mehta, published by Parshvanath Research Institute, Varanasi, 1993.

apprehend all the characteristics of an object, idea or proposition.

3. In view of the above, we should be cautious in reacting to a thing or a thought which we encounter in life.
4. We should make an objective and unbiased approach towards each situation or idea.
5. Prudence dictates that our view, based on limited data and capability cannot be absolute. It may be true to some extent or it can even be untrue if looked at from some other perspective.

The above approach of relativism (SYAADAVAAD) implies that all knowledge is relative. The Sanskrit word SYAAD ordinarily means 'might be' but it is best rendered as 'in some respect' in Jain usage.[2] S. N. Dasgupta observes, "This (SYAAD ASTI - positive aspect) will indicate that the affirmation is only relative, made somehow, from some point of view and under some reservations and not in any sense absolute. There is no judgement which is absolutely true, and no judgement which is absolutely false. All judgements are true in some sense and false in another."[3] It is important to point out that the word 'SYAAD' is not used to express doubt but it is employed to avoid one-sided assertions. It is used to show that our knowledge about the manifold aspects of a thing is limited. Thus relativism is based on the premise that every proposition is only relatively true. It all depends on the particular aspect from which we appreciate that proposition. Since the various propositions are related to many different circumstances, our assertions are based on the particular situations in which we view them. Since our view is through a limited aperture, we can not see all aspects and hence it is appropriate to avoid absolute assertions.

Dr. S. Radhakrishnan writes, "Attributes which are contradictory in the abstract, coexist in life and experience. The tree is moving in that its branches are moving, and it is not moving since it is fixed to a place in the ground. It is necessary for us to know a thing clearly and distinctly, in its self existence as well as in its relations to other objects."[4] Here is another example from modern science. Consider the scientific fact that a moving electric charge produces a magnetic field while an electric charge at rest does not. Accordingly, if a

---

2 The Jaina Path of Purification by Dr. Padmanabh S. Jaini, published by Motilal Banarsidass, Delhi, 1979, page 94.

3 A History of Indian Philosophy by S. N. Dasgupta, published by Cambridge University Press, 1963, Volume 1, page 179.

4 Indian Philosophy, Volume 1, published by The Macmillan Company, New York, 1962, page 304.

charged sphere is being carried in a spacecraft, the astronauts will not detect any magnetic field around the sphere while the scientists on earth will find that the charged sphere in motion is producing a magnetic field.[5] Thus the same charged sphere is producing a magnetic field when observed from one vantage point (earth) because it is in motion relative to the earth while it is not producing any magnetic field observed from another vantage point (spacecraft).

Similar statements can be made about our observations relating to time and space and about every human experience. It is a matter of our daily experience that an object which gives pleasure to us under certain circumstances, becomes boring under different circumstances. Modern scientists do not claim to have a complete and exhaustive knowledge of the universe and the laws that govern it. Scientific knowledge progresses as more and more research is done. Scientific truths are thus partial and relative as are the truths about our life experiences. Nevertheless, relative truth is undoubtedly useful. In the field of spiritualism, it is the stepping stone to the ultimate truth.

### Importance of Negative

According to the Jain concept of relativism, it is important to bear in mind that when we make a positive assertion about a thing, there is an implied negative, which, if not taken into account properly, may create confusion. For instance, a man is a father to his sons and daughters but not to his own father or to other individuals. He is different to different individuals in his social relationships. So when his parenthood is referred to, it is true only in relation to his children but not true in relation to his wife or friends. Both these positive and negative aspects are important for a proper description of that man. The statement about parenthood has a positive aspect (SYAAD ASTI) and simultaneously a negative aspect (SYAAD NAASTI). Both positive and negative aspects are essential for identifying an object properly. The two aspects imply what the object is and what it is not. The Jain logic also admits another aspect: it implies that an object is inexpressible (AVAKTAVYA). Combinations of these three aspects lead to the theory of seven predicates (SAPTABHANGI) as will be described later.

### Principle of Multiplicity of Viewpoints

Acharya Hemchandra equates relativism (SYAADAVAAD) with the

5 Cosmology - Old And New by Prof. G. R. Jain, published by Bharatiya Jnaanpith, New Delhi, 1975, page ix.

principle of multiplicity of viewpoints (ANEKAANTAVAAD).[6] The Sanskrit word ANEKAANT implies a multitude of aspects. Thus SYAADAVAAD and NAYAVAAD (theory of partial truths) are corollaries of ANEKAANTAVAAD.[7] We observe that the various objects in the universe continuously undergo the processes of creation (UTPAAD) and destruction (VYAYA) while they maintain their permanence (DHROVYA - intrinsic nature). Based on this observation, the Jain thinkers concluded that every object is permanent as well as transitory. On the surface, this appears to be contradictory. Even great scholars like Shankar and Ramanuj have pointed out such contradictions. However, such contradictions can be understood by applying the doctrine of relativism. The contradictions are seen in reference to the same aspect and in the same sense and time. Since reality is multifold and ever changing, it has to be examined from different viewpoints. An object is permanent considering its substratum which remains constant and it is transitory because it continuously undergoes transformations.

Suppose a potter takes a lump of clay and makes a jug. Before the jug has a chance to dry, he changes his mind, breaks the jug and makes a bowl out of the clay. In this process, the substance, clay has remained unchanged. From this point of view, an object maintains its permanence. However, the forms of the clay have been changed from a lump to a jug and finally to a bowl. From this aspect, an object is transitory. Dr. A. N. Upadhye comments, "This doctrine of seven-fold predication (SAPTABHANGI) is often misunderstood and misrepresented by idealists who have not been able to appreciate the metaphysical basis and intellectual approach. It reminds one of the realistic relativists of the West such as Whitehead and others. The Jain logician is neither a skeptic nor an agnostic; but he is a realist working with sound common sense. He does not want to ignore the relative or conditional character of the judgement arising out of the very nature of the object of knowledge."[8]

### Is Self Permanent Or Transitory?

In the field of metaphysics, the various schools of thought present different views of the nature of "self" (soul). For example, the Vedantists believe that all beings in the universe are BRAHMA, the super-self that is permanent and the material things have no reality

6 SYAADITYAVYAYAMANEKAATAH DYOTAKAM.

7 The Jaina Path of Purification, page 97.

8 Article on Jainism published in "Cultural History of India", edited by A. L. Basham, Clarendon Press, Oxford 1975, page 105.

as they are transitory in nature. The Buddhists, on the other hand, say that everything including the super self is transitory and is constantly changing. These are two extreme views as they concentrate only on a particular aspect to the exclusion of the other aspect. Jainism says that both are relatively correct from the viewpoint from which they see nature and both are incorrect in as much as they fail to take the comprehensive view of all aspects involved. The Jains would call to aid their doctrine of SYAADAVAAD. From the point of view of substance, all things in the universe (including the souls) are permanent (SYAAD ASTI, the positive aspect) and from the point of view of transformations or modes (PARYAAYAs), everything is transitory (SYAAD NAASTI, the negative aspect). A confluence of the two views is that a substance and its modes should be considered as a whole and both the attributes (permanent as well as transitory nature) should be taken into account in order to adequately comprehend reality. This aspect is called confluence of positive and negative aspects (SYAAD ASTI-NAASTI).

**Theory of Seven Predicates** (SAPTABHANGI)

The following theory of seven predicates (SAPTABHANGI) is obtained by combining the positive aspect (ASTI), the negative aspect (NAASTI) and the aspect of inexpressibility (AVAKTAVYA). The seven predicates have been illustrated with the help of an example.

1. The positive aspect (SYAAD ASTI): Violence is inadmissible in a civilized society because, in general, it leads to further violence.
2. The negative aspect (SYAAD NAASTI): Violence may be necessary against an aggressor who molests a helpless woman.
3. The confluence of positive and negative aspects (SYAAD ASTI-NAASTI): It is inadmissible to commit violence because it is a breach of morals; but it may be necessary in case of a breach of the laws of society.
4. The inexpressible aspect (SYAAD AVAKTAVYA): It is not possible to make a blanket statement on inadmissibility or necessity of violence. Each instance has to be judged based on the circumstances.
5. The confluence of positive and inexpressible aspects (SYAAD ASTI-AVAKTAVYA): Violence is inadmissible but such a statement cannot be made for all circumstances.
6. The confluence of negative and inexpressible aspects (SYAAD NAASTI-AVAKTAVYA): Violence may be necessary but such a statement cannot be made for all circumstances.
7. The confluence of positive, negative and inexpressible aspects

(SYAAD ASTI-NAASTI-AVAKTAVYA): Violence is inadmissible but there are circumstances when it may be necessary. However, no affirmative or negative statement can be made for all times and circumstances.

The above example presents a very rough application of the theory of seven predicates. It lacks many details and sophistication. To quote Eliot, "The essence of the doctrine (of SYAADAVAAD) so far as one can disentangle it from scholastic terminology, seems just, for it amounts to this, that as to matters of experience it is impossible to formulate the whole and complete truth, and as to matters which transcend experience, language is inadequate."[9]

Regarding the above example, it should be pointed out that our belief in the supremacy of nonviolence should not be compromised in making decisions based on the principle of multiplicity of viewpoints. All physical and mental violence performed under any circumstances leads to the influx and bondage of undesirable karma (PAAP). Moreover, violence leads to violence and, in general, it does not lead to an overall welfare of any society. The most desirable approach is to avoid situations which may lead to violence.

The Jain thinkers have applied the approach of seven predicates to explain the various aspects of reality relating to soul, its identity, character and immortality. In fact, this approach of relativism permeates every basic principle of the Jain philosophy.

**Relevance of Relativism to Society**

The doctrine of relativism is extremely useful in everyday life. It provides a rational synthesis of the various views of a given situation or proposition and rejects the assertions of bare absolutes. Mahatma Gandhi held the principle of multiplicity of viewpoints in high esteem. In 1926, he observed:[10]

"It has been my experience that I am always true (correct) from my point of view, and often wrong from the point of view of my honest critics. I know we are both right from our respective points of view."

Mahatma Gandhi continues, "I very much like this doctrine of the manyness of reality. It is this doctrine that has taught me to judge a Mussulman from his standpoint and a Christian from his. . . . From the platform of the Jains, I prove the non-creative aspect of God, and

---

9 Outlines of Jainism by S. Gopalan, published by Wiley Eastern Ltd., New Delhi, 1973, page 156.

10 The editorial by Mahatma Gandhi in the Journal 'Young India', January 26, 1926. Reprinted in M. K. Gandhi, 'Truth is God', Ahmedabad, India, 1955, page 11.

from that of Ramanuj, the creative aspect. As a matter of fact, we are all thinking of the unthinkable, describing the indescribable, seeking to know the unknown, and that is why our speech falters, is inadequate, and even often contradictory."

The German philosopher Immanual Kant has expressed similar thoughts in the following words:[11]

"Formerly, I viewed human common sense only from the standpoint of my own; now I put myself into the position of another's reason outside of myself, and observe my judgements, together with their most secret causes, from the point of view of others. It is true that the comparison of both observations results in pronounced parallaxes. But it is the only means of preventing the optical delusion, and of putting the concept of the power of knowledge in human nature into its true place."

History of all conflicts and confrontations in the world is the history of intolerance born out of ignorance and misunderstanding. This is also true of the differences between Digambars and Shwetambars. We Jains should study the basic principles of our religion to understand that the differences between the various groups are insignificant and irrelevant. If Jains follow the principle of multiplicity of viewpoints in their conduct, there will be fewer conflicts in our lives and in our dealings with others. Our society will be better and other groups will learn the significance of the Jain principles.

* * * * * * *

Advocates of religion often suffer from dogmatism. They may agree that what they have known is not absolute truth, but they insist that what others believe is absolutely wrong. The clash between sects is a result of this dogmatism.

- Acharya Shri Mahaprajna

* * * * * * *

---

11 The Philosophy of Kant: Immanuel Kant's Moral and Political Writings, edited by C. J. Fredrich, Modern Library, New York, 1949, page 15.

Statue of Gommateshwar Bahubali at Shravanabelgola
On the Occasion of MAHAMASTAKAABHISHEK
(Great Head-anointing Ceremony)

# The History Of Jainism: A Brief Survey

by Prof. Padmanabh S. Jaini[1]

## Prehistorical

Of the twenty-four TEERTHANKARs (JINs) of our time, the first twenty-two TEERTHANKARs, Rishabh through Neminath belong to the prehistoric period. These TEERTHANKARs belong to a period for which corroborating evidence is not available. According to the Jain scriptures, the twenty-third TEERTHANKAR Parshvanath was born 84,000 years after the NIRVANA of Neminath. The twenty-fourth TEERTHANKAR Vardhamaan Mahaveer was born 250 years after the NIRVANA of Parshvanath.

## Historical

The twenty-third TEERTHANKAR Parshvanath was born in 949 B.C. in Varanasi in the state of Uttar Pradesh. In 849 B.C., at the age of one hundred years, Bhagwaan Parshvanath attained NIRVANA at Sammed Shikhar in the state of Bihar.

Vardhamaan Mahaveer, born in 599 B.C., was a senior contemporary of Gautam Buddha. Vardhamaan Mahaveer is not mentioned in any Brahminical texts. The most ancient designation applied to Mahaveer, in both the Jain and the Buddhist literature is NIGGANTH (free from bonds) NAATPUTTA (son of NAATRA clan). His name or title Mahaveer (meaning the great hero) by which he is now known, is not found in the Buddhist texts. Mahaveer's mendicant disciples were called NIGGANTHs. His lay disciples were called NIGGANTH-SHRAAVAKs/SHRAAVIKAs or UPAASAKAs/UPAASIKAs. The designation Jain (i.e. followers of JIN) is not attested before the 5th century A.D.

Mahaveer was born at Kundgram[2], in the princely state of Vaishali in North Bihar. His parents, King Siddharth and Queen Trishala, were followers of Bhagwaan Parshvanath. When Mahaveer was thirty years old, he renounced the household and became a mendicant (follower of the path of NIGGANTH). After twelve years of severe asceticism, at the age of forty-two, Mahaveer attained omniscience (KEVAL JNAAN). He reinstated the religious system of NIGGANTHs and thus became a TEERTHANKAR (JIN). He attained NIRVANA

1 Lecture delivered at the Sixth JAINA Biennial Convention, Stanford University, July 4-6, 1991.

2 According to some sources, the name of Mahaveer's birth place is Kshatriyakund.

in 527 B.C. at the age of seventy-two at Pavapuri, near Patna (Bihar). At the time of his NIRVANA, his TEERTH (community of adherents) is said to have consisted of 14,000 monks (SADHUs) led by his chief interpreter (GANADHAR, the head of the order) Gautam Swami, 36,000 nuns (SADHVIs) led by Chandana (GANINI, the chief nun), one hundred thousand SHRAAVAKs and three hundred thousand SHRAAVIKAs (male and female householders who had assumed the rules of conduct appropriate to the follower of a NIGGANTH). The immediate successors to Mahaveer were his two interpreters, Gautam and Sudharm, and the latter's disciple Jambu. They organized the teachings of Mahaveer into twelve main texts (called the DVAADASHAANG SUTRA) which were transmitted to the mendicant disciples in an oral tradition.

**Split in the mendicant community**

About 200 years after Mahaveer's NIRVANA, the until then unified mendicant order of NIGGANTHs, seems to have broken into two major groups. This event reportedly began at Patliputra (Patna, Bihar) during the reign of the first Mauryan Emperor Chandragupta, a contemporary of Alexander the Great (about 327 B.C.). The head of the mendicant community at that time was Bhadrabahu I. Later accounts indicate that during that period a council of monks was held at Patliputra in the absence of Bhadrabahu under the leadership of his disciple Sthulabhadra to collect the scriptures that were scattered in various recensions (slightly different versions) due to the oral tradition. According to one account, Bhadrabahu had migrated to the South with many disciples due to a severe drought in Magadh (Bihar). According to another, he was away in Nepal engaged in meditation and hence was not able to participate in the council. This council reportedly resulted in a major split in the community of NIGGANTH monks, one faction accepting the scriptures organized by Sthulabhadra while the other rejecting their authenticity. One point of controversy seems to pertain to wearing of clothes by monks; the followers of Bhadrabahu claiming that NIGGANTH monks should not wear clothes, while those of Sthulabhadra maintaining that monks can wear clothes and that essential items such as clothes do not constitute possessions (PARIGRAH).[3] Eventually, towards the beginning of the Christian

3 Some scholars hold this view while others, on the basis of Gautam-Kesi dialogue contained in the UTTTARAADHYAYAN SUTRA (a scripture which is traditionally accepted by Shwetambars), are of the opinion that even at the time of Bhagwaan Parshvanath, NIGGANTHs could wear

era, this dispute gave rise to two main groups of Jain mendicants, the ACHELAKs (without clothes) and SACHELAKs (with clothes). The subsequent history of Jainism is essentially a history of these two groups called, respectively, Digambar (which literally means sky-clad) and Shwetambar (which literally means clad in white). The lay society was also divided accordingly and came to be known by the same designations, i.e., Digambars and Shwetambars. Both groups have spread far and wide in the vast land of India and have lived side by side for centuries with very little interaction between them.

The migration of the Jain monks together with their followers took place along two major trade routes of ancient India. In the east, the route went from Patna (Bihar) to Orissa and then south to Andhra Pradesh, Karnatak and Tamilnadu. The Digambars claim that Bhadrabahu and his disciples followed this route and established their mendicant order (SANGH) in these distant places. The first inscriptional evidence for such a migration is provided by the Jain king Khaaravel, who ruled around 150 B.C., from Udayagiri, near the modern city of Bhuvaneshvar in Orissa. The route to the west went parallel to the river Ganges and terminated in Mathura on the banks of the river Yamuna. A large scale migration of Jains (and Buddhists) took place along this route after the fall of the Ashokan empire in 150 B.C. at the hands of Pushyamitra Sunga. Henceforth Jains almost disappeared from Magadh, the land of Mahaveer, but greatly flourished in Mathura. Excavations in Mathura (known as Kankaali Teela excavations) have yielded a large number of Jain monuments and inscriptions dating from about 150 B.C. to 500 A.D. and some images of TEERTHANKARs attended by monks, nuns and lay devotees.[4]

From Mathura, the Jains of both groups made rapid progress towards the south and the west, to Rajasthan, Malwa and Gujarat, and by the second century A.D., they were well established at Valabhi, the capital city of Saurashtra (near modern Junagarh). Here the Digambar acharyas, Pushpadant and Bhootabali compiled the remnants of their scriptures called the SHATAKHANDA-AGAM in 150 A.D.

---

clothes. See, for example, 'A History of the Jainas' by Ashim Kumar Roy, Gitanjali Publishing House, New Delhi, 1984, page 21. For an examination of Gautam-Kesi dialogue, see 'The Jaina Path of Purification' by P. S. Jaini, University of California Press, 1979, pages 14-20.

4 For a detailed account see 'A History of the Jainas' by Ashim Kumar Roy, Gitanjali Publishing House, New Delhi, 1984, pages 77-82. On page 81, A. K. Roy writes, "It is likely, however, that the Shwetambar-Digambar split had not become clear-cut by that time."

received from their teacher Acharya Dharasen who was of the lineage of Acharya Bhadrabahu. Valabhi was also the city where the entire scriptures (AGAMs) of the Shwetambar tradition were reorganized and written down on palm-leaves under the supervision of Acharya Devaardhigani Kshamaashraman in the year 453 A.D. We owe this date to KALPASUTRA, a Shwetambar text about the 'Lives of the JINs' (JINACHARITA), which states: After his (i.e. Mahaveer's) NIRVANA nine centuries have now elapsed; of the tenth century this is the eightieth year.' The year 980 of the VEER-NIRVANA SAMVAT (calendar), the earliest historical era of India recorded here, helps us establish the dates of Mahaveer as 599-527 B.C.

Though the Digambars settled in large numbers in many cities of Rajasthan, Malwa and Gujarat, their literary activities flourished more in the South. They did not accept the scriptures recognized by the Shwetambars and needed to produce the scriptures of their own (based on the oral tradition). The need was fulfilled by Acharya Kundkund of the Bhadrabahu lineage who was probably from Andhra and lived in the second century A.D. Kundkund composed several important short texts in Prakrit described as essence (SAAR): the SAMAYASAAR (essence of self-realization), the PRAVACHANASAAR (essence of teaching) and so on and so forth. Acharya Umaswami (also called Umaswati), in about 200 A.D., produced the most systematized summary of the entire doctrine in the work called TATTVAARTH SUTRA. It should be noted that Umaswati has been claimed by the Shwetambars also as their own. Thus the TATTVAARTH SUTRA remains to this day the only text acceptable to both sects.[5] In addition to the voluminous commentaries to the works mentioned above, eminent acharyas such as Samant Bhadra (5th century A.D.), Akalanka (7th century A.D.) and Veersen (8th century A.D.) produced independent treatises on Jain philosophy. Here one must also mention the MAHAPURAAN by Acharya Jinasen (A.D. 770-850) completed by his disciple Gunabhadra, the main source for the Digambar narratives about the twenty-four TEERTHANKARs and other illustrious figures of the Jain tradition. Jinasen was also influential in the court of the Rashtrakoot kings. During this time, several magnificent caves were excavated in the hills of Ellora (near Aurangabad, Maharashtra). During the same period, a Jain named Jinadattaraya carved out a small kingdom at a place now known as Humcha where he built great temples

5 This corroborates that the doctrine accepted by both Digambars and Shwetambars is the same, a fact accepted by many scholars. See Jain Study Circular, July 1991, pages 14-15, for some details. - D.C.J.

of JINs and established a shrine for Padmavati, a guardian-deity (SHAASAN DEVI) of Parshvanath. The most glorious achievement, however, of the Jains of Karnatak was the erection of the colossal image of Bahubali, about 60 feet tall, on the mountain top of Shravanabelgola. This image was commissioned by Chamundaraya, a prominent Jain general in the Ganga Kingdom, in 948 A.D., at the instruction of Acharya Nemichandra. Shravanabelgola also served as one of the major centers for the libraries of scriptures (BHANDAARs) supervised by the line of BHATTAARAKs (the teachers and administrators) beginning with Panditadev (in 1398 A.D.) and remains to this day a major place of Jain pilgrimage.

We may now return to the North where the Jains flourished as great leaders of the mercantile communities. Valabhi fell to the Arabs in 789 A.D. and the capital was moved to Anahilawad Patan in 850 A.D. There the Shwetambar Jains moved into positions of great influence. The great Acharya Hemchandra spent his long life (1088-1173 A.D.) in this city where he composed his voluminous TRISHASHTHI-SHALAAKAPURUSH CHARIT (lives of the sixty-three illustrious persons). He was instrumental in converting to Jainism the Shaivite (follower of Shiva) King Kumarpal, ruler of Gujarat between 1143-1174 A.D. and obtained from him a proclamation of protection for animals in his kingdom (AMAARI). Jain laymen also served their kings with distinction in various offices. Mention must be made of the Jain householder Vastupal (1190-1240 A.D.), a minister of King Veeradhaval at Dhavalakka (near Ahmedabad - a feudatory of Patan) who built majestic temples on Mount Girnar in Saurashtra. His younger brother Tejpal (the administrator of Khambat) built the magnificent marble temples on Mount Abu in 1231 A.D.

**Reform movements in Rajasthan and Gujarat**

The temple building activities of the Jains described above were no doubt inspired by their devotion to the teachings of the JINs. Such acts of devotion, however, demanded a close participation of the mendicants in consecrating the images and in performing other rituals beneficial to the laymen. This participation eventually created a whole class of renegade monks, called YATIs (clerics), who were regarded as experts in temple rituals. Acharya Haribhadra (750 A.D.) of Rajasthan, author of the AVASHYAK Commentary and the SHADDARSHAN SAMUCHCHAYA, was the first to notice the excesses of these temple-dwelling (CHAITYAVAASI) Shwetambar monks and condemned their impropriety in living in affluence contrary to the rules of mendicancy. But it would be several centuries before a concerted effort to purify the order of monks would start. The credit for initiating this effort goes to Vardhamaan Suri (1026 A.D.) and his successors, notably, Jineshvar Suri and Jinadatta Suri (in about 1150 A.D.), popularly known as Dada. The latter founded a sect called KHARATARA (the pure ones) which not only enforced strict laws of mendicancy but also converted thousands of non-Jains in Punjab, Haryana, Rajasthan and Saurashtra to Jainism.

In 1451 A.D., several traditional Shwetambar monks of Gujarat belonging to the TAPAAGACHCHHA group split and followed the leadership of a Jain layman Lonka Shaha of Ahmedabad. The first monk of this new group was Bhanaji in 1474 A.D. He was joined by six other monks, all of the Oswal community which had migrated to Gujarat from Osia in Marwar, Rajasthan. This group of reformist monks was referred to as LONKA GACHCHHA. They became the forerunners of what came to be known as the STHAANAKAVAASI (meaning dwellers in halls) group, a designation which distinguished them from the CHAITYAVAASI (DERAAVAASI, temple dweller) monks. The STHAANAKAVAASIs introduced strict rules of residence for their mendicants, began the use of a piece of cloth (MUHAPATTI) against the mouth to minimize the violence of small organisms. They also maintain that the worship of images of the JINs is not sanctioned in the scriptures. Eventually, their lay followers also adopted this belief and disassociated themselves from the monks who supported image worship. A subgroup of the STHAANAKAVAASI mendicants is called TERA PANTH (group of thirteen, the original number of dissenting monks). It was founded by Acharya Bhikshu (1727-1802 A.D.) of Jodhpur (popularly called Muni Bhikanji) who separated from his STHAANAKAVAASI teacher Muni Raghunathji (1709-1789 A.D.), apparently because he disagreed with his teacher on the validity of the acts of compassion such as feeding the non-mendicant poor.[6]

Although the splits were in the mendicant community, the activities of these reform movements had their desired effect on the main-stream Shwetambar (now known as Shwetambar Murtipujak, i.e., image worshiper) populace. Many acharyas of TAPAAGACHCHHA were able to attract the attention even of the Moslem rulers by their scholarship and asceticism. Noteworthy among these is Hiravijaya Suri of the TAPAAGACHCHHA, who was one of the instructors of the Moghul Emperor Akbar (1556-1605 A.D.) and obtained from him a

6 Another view is that Bhikhanji stressed thirteen virtues, i.e. five vows (VRATs), conscientiousness in five activities (SAMITIs) and self-restraint of body, speech and mind (GUPTIs). - D. C. J.

proclamation in 1583 A.D. for the protection of animals (AMAARI) during PARYUSHAN, the celebration of spiritual awareness, which is the most sacred occasion for the Jain community.

That was the time when North India gave birth to several great poet-saints, notably, Kabir (1440-1518 A.D.), Guru Nanak (1469-1539 A.D.), Mirabai (1470-1518 A.D.), and Tulsidas (1532-1623 A.D.). Their ardently devotional songs exerted tremendous influence on both the lay and the mendicant Jains, who did not accept the theory of God, the Creator, and had professed salvation through self-effort alone. These theistic movements directed several Jain thinkers to go beyond the narrow confines of sectarian monasticism in search of 'self-realization' (ATMA-ANUBHAV), without compromising the basic Jain doctrine of salvation. Two prominent names may be mentioned in this connection.

The first one was a great poet called Anandaghan (1613-1673 A.D.), a Jain mendicant of the TAPAAGACHCHHA. Anandaghan provided the Jains with new means of relishing the spiritual flavor hidden behind their daily temple rituals through his devotional songs (STOTRAs) in Rajasthani dialect addressed to the twenty-four JINs.

The second person was not even a monk but a merchant of modest means and a poet, called Banarsidas (1587-1644 A.D.) of Agra belonging to the Shwetambar TAPAAGACHCHHA group. His contact with some learned merchants of the Digambar group led him to the discovery of Acharya Kundkund's SAMAYASAAR mentioned above. He was impressed by the emphasis laid in this ancient text on the primacy of 'self-realization' in the life of a Jain aspirant and so he composed a marvelous rendering of it in Hindi entitled 'SAMAYASAAR NAATAK'.

It is hard to measure the impact of this lyrical composition on the succeeding generations of Jains. It was felt as far away as a small town called Vavaania in Saurashtra and molded the life of another young poet called Rajchandra Mehta, known to us today as Shrimad Rajchandra. In his short life (1867-1901 A.D.) he was to attain world-wide fame as a friend and unique spiritual master of Mahatma Gandhi. Rajchandra was a fine product of a confluence of two major spiritual streams of India. He was born into a staunch Vaishnav family but his mother was a Jain of the STHAANAKAVAASI persuasion. He was married, had four children, and had been very successful in his occupation as a jeweller. In his childhood, he had lived near a Jain monastery (UPAASHRAYA) but he gained his instruction in Jainism by his own wide reading of such texts as ACHAARAANG SUTRA,

UTTARAADHYAYAN SUTRA, DRAVYA SANGRAH, MOKSHAMAARG PRAKAASHAK and SAMAYASAAR. He did not hesitate in the worship of images of the JINs when he realized that it was beneficial for his meditative activities. His broadened vision helped him overcome the narrow approaches of the sects and to declare boldly: "Please do not lose sight of this: I do not belong to any GACHCHHA (group); I belong to ATMAN (soul)." He did not renounce the household life but was, by his spiritual magnetism, able to inspire devotion in a small group of STHAANAKAVAASI monks of long standing. For the same reason, he attracted the attention of the young lawyer Mohandas Gandhi, who, assailed by doubt created by Christian missionaries about his religion, corresponded with Shrimad Rajchandra from South Africa during the years 1894-96 and through this communication confirmed his own faith. It is indeed a great tribute to the spirit of multiplicity of viewpoints (ANEKAANT) shown by Shrimad Rajchandra, when Mahatma Gandhi, recalling his old days said: "In my moments of spiritual crisis . . . he was my refuge."

These are a few glimpses of the history of Jainism.

**Suggested Reading**

1. The Jaina Path of Purification by Padmanabh S. Jaini, published by University of California Press, 1979.
2. Gender and Salvation by Padmanabh S. Jaini, published by University of California Press, 1991.
3. Jaina Yoga by R. Williams, Motilal Banarsidass, Delhi, 1989.

* * * * * * *

Those who praise their own faith, disparage their opponents, and possess malice against them will remain confined to the cycle of birth and death.

- SUTRAKRITAANG

The second earliest Jain scripture (2nd century B.C.)

* * * * * * *

# The Philosophical Foundation of Religious Tolerance in Jainism

by Dr. Sagarmal Jain[1]

## What is True Religion?

The basic purpose of all religions is to ensure peace and happiness for the individual and to establish harmony within human society. However, as is known from history, countless wars have been fought in the name of religion. Religion thus remains accused of inestimable bloodshed of mankind. Indeed, it is not the religion but the fundamentalists, extremists and the so-called men of religion with rigid outlooks who are responsible for the horrible consequences. These days religion is largely shoved into the background or at best used to serve political ideologies. If one believes that only his faith, his mode of worship and his political ideologies are the right means for securing peace and happiness for mankind, then he can not be tolerant of the viewpoint of others.

Can religion as a class, of which Jainism is a part, meet the challenge of our times? A religion can not support violence, intolerance and fanatical behavior. Thus it can not condone the ignominious acts committed in the name of religion by religious leaders who want to serve their vested interests. The barbarism committed in the past and perpetrated these days in the name of religion is due largely to the intolerance and fanaticism of the so-called religious leaders and their ignorant followers. The only way to free oneself from this sordid situation is to comprehend the true nature of religion and to develop toleranc: toward and respect for others' ideologies and faiths.

For Jains, the true practice of religion consists of equanimity and nonviolence. ACHAARAANG SUTRA, the earliest Jain text of late 4th century B.C., states: Equanimity is the essence of religion and observance of nonviolence is its external exposition or a social aspect of religion. Jainism teaches us peace, harmony and tolerance. In Jainism one hardly comes across instances of religious conflict involving violence and bloodshed. At most one finds some instances of disputes and strongly worded debates concerning ideological differences. In many cases, Jain scholars, while opposing other

1 An abridged version of a paper read at the Assembly of World Religions, published in Lala Harjasrai Commemoration Volume, P. V. Research Institute, Varanasi 1987, pages 43-56

ideologies and religious standpoints, admitted that the opponent's convictions may also be valid from a certain standpoint.

### Passionate Regard (Attachment): The Root Of Intolerance

Blind faith is the principal cause of fanaticism and intolerance. It results from passionate attachment and hence uncritical outlook. Indeed, in Jain literature, blind faith (DARSHAN MOHA/DRISHTIRAAG) has been enumerated as one type of passionate attachment. Passionate attachment (MOORCHHA) is caused by delusion. It results in perverse attitude and karmic bondage. Blind faith leads one to inculcate the attitude of a strong bias toward one's own religion and intolerance of other religions. Non-attachment is considered a precondition for the right attitude or perception (SAMYAK DARSHAN). Dr. Tatia writes,[2] "Attachment and hatred are two great enemies of philosophical thinking. Truth can reveal itself to an impartial thinker." One who is impartial and unbiased can perceive the truth of his opponent's ideology and faith. Thus he can have deference to them. Intense attachment invariably generates blind adherence to religious leaders, dogmas, doctrines and rituals. It leads to intolerance.[3]

Jainism holds that the slightest and even pious attachment towards the TEERTHANKARs, the path and the scripture is a hindrance to a seeker of truth and spiritual uplift. Gautam Swami, the chief disciple and interpreter of Mahaveer, failed to attain omniscience in the lifetime of Bhagwaan Mahaveer on account of pious attachment to his master. Attachment, be it pious or impious, cannot be without aversion or repulsion. Attachment results in blind faith and superstition while repulsion leads to intolerant conduct. Jains, therefore, lay stress on the elimination of attachment, the root cause of bias and intolerance.

### Reason: The Checkpoint Of Blind Faith

"The differences in the religious ideologies should be critically evaluated through the faculty of reasoning," says the ancient Jain text, UTTARAADHYAYAN SUTRA.[4] This means that SAMYAK DARSHAN (rational perception), one of the three jewels of Jainism, which is commonly referred to as right faith is not blind faith. It is accompanied by rational knowledge, knowledge acquired through critical reasoning. According to Jain thinkers, reason and faith (rational perception) are complementary and there is no contention

2 N. M. Tatia, Studies in Jaina Philosophy, P. V. Research Institute, Varanasi, 1958, page 22.

3 This is the present state of the various groups among Jains. - D. C. J.

4 Chapter 23, couplet 25.

between them. They hold that religious codes and rituals should be critically analyzed.

If one maintains that religion is solely based on faith and there is no place for reason in it, then he will invariably develop an outlook that only his prophet, religion and scripture are true and others' religions, prophets and scriptures are false. He will also believe that his prophet is the only savior of mankind; his mode of worship is the only way of experiencing the bliss and the laws of his scripture are the only right ones.[5] Thus he remains incompetent in making a critical estimate of his religious prescriptions. One who maintains that reason also plays an important role in the religious life, will critically evaluate the pros and cons of religious prescriptions, rituals and dogmas. An 'attached' or biased person believes in the dictum 'mine is true' while the 'detached' or unbiased person believes in the dictum 'truth is mine'.

Gunaratnasuri (early 15th century A.D.) has written,[6] "A biased person tries to justify whatever he has already accepted while an unprejudiced person accepts what he feels is logically justified." Jainism supports rational thinking.[7] Acharya Haribhadrasuri (about third quarter of 8th century A.D.) says,[8] "I possess no bias for Bhagwaan Mahaveer and no prejudice against Kapil and other saints and thinkers. Whosoever is logical and rational ought to be accepted." Thus if we are rational, there will hardly be any room for intolerance.

## Non-Absolutism: The Philosophical Basis For Tolerance

Dogmatism and fanaticism are the born children of absolutism. An extremist holds that his faith is absolutely true and what others say is false, while a relativist is of the view that he and his opponent both may be correct if viewed from two different angles. Thus a relativist adopts a tolerant outlook towards other faiths and ideologies. The Jain doctrine of ANEKAANTAVAAD (non-absolutism) forms the basis for

---

5 It is ironic that we hear such pronouncements about Jainism at Jain functions, celebrations and conferences. - D. C. J.

6 SADDARSANASAMUCCAYA of Haribhadrasuri, including TARKA RAHASYA DIPIKA by Gunaratnasuri, edited by Dr. Mahendra Kumar Jain Nyayacharya, Bharatiya Jnanpith, New Delhi, 1989, page 461.

7 In some instances, Jains, young and old, make decisions and take actions that may compromise the principles of Jainism. It is improper to seek or present rationale for such actions on the basis of relativism. - D. C. J.

8 LOKATATTVANIRNAYA, verse 38, Jain Granth Prakashak Sabha, Ahmedabad, Vikram 1994.

the concept of tolerance. Jains believe in nonviolence. Absolutism hurts the feelings of others and thus it constitutes violence of thought. A nonviolent search for truth entails non-absolutism.

Jain thinkers hold the view that reality is complex. It has many facets, various attributes and various modes. It can be viewed and understood from different angles and thus various judgements may be made about it. Even two contradictory statements about an object may hold true. Since we have finite capability, we can know or experience only a few facets of reality at one time. The reality in its totality cannot be grasped by us. Only a universal observer (omniscient) can comprehend it completely. Yet even for an omniscient it is impossible to know it and explain it without a standpoint or a viewpoint.[9] This premise can be understood from the following example. Suppose everyone of us has a camera for photographing a tree and we all use it. We can have hundreds of photographs but still we will find a considerable portion of the tree missing from each photograph. Further, the photographs will differ from each other unless they are taken from the same angle. The same is true about human beings having diverse understanding and knowledge. We can have only a partial and relative view of reality. It is impossible for us to know and describe reality without an angle or viewpoint. While the picture of reality taken from each viewpoint is true, it is only partial and relative. On the basis of partial and relative view of reality, how can we claim the right to discard the views of our opponents as totally false? Thus Jain thinkers teach us to accept and respect the truth-value of our opponents' viewpoints.

Non-absolutism of Jains prevents the individual from being dogmatic and one-sided in approach. It impels us to adopt a broad outlook and have an open mind which can help us resolve the conflicts that emerge from differences in ideologies and faiths. Prof. Satkari Mookherjee observed that Jains do not believe in the extremist a priori logic of the absolutists. He writes,[10] "Pragmatically considered, this logical attitude (of absolutism) breeds dogmatism, and if carried a step further, engenders fanaticism, the worst and the vilest passion of human heart." For those who believe in non-absolutism, the views of all the opponents are also true. Acharya Siddhasen Diwakar (5th century A.D.) writes,[11] "All schools of

9 AVASHYAK NIRYUKTI, 544; VISHESHAAVASHYAK BHAASHYA, 2748, L. D. Institute of Indology, Ahmehabad, 1968.

10 Foundation of World Peace, Ahimsa and Anekant, Vaishali Institute Research Bulletin No. 1, page 229.

thought are valid when they are understood from their own standpoint and insofar as they do not discard the truth-value of others. The knower of non-absolutism does not divide them into true and false. They become false when they discard the truth-value of others." It is this broader outlook of non-absolutism that makes Jains tolerant.

While expounding the tolerant outlook of the Jains, Upaadhyaaya Yashovijay (17th century A.D.) mentioned,[12] "A true non-absolutist does not have disdain for any faith. He treats all faiths equally like a father to his sons, for a non-absolutist does not have any prejudicial and biased outlook. A true believer in SYAADAVAAD (non-absolutism) pays equal regard to all faiths. To remain impartial towards all faiths is the essence of being religious. A little knowledge which induces a person to be impartial is more worthwhile than the unilateral vast knowledge of scriptures."

**Non-Personalism: A Keystone For Tolerance**

It is person-worship that makes our minds biased and intolerant. Jainism assails person-cult. For the Jains, the object of veneration and worship is not a person but the quality of being perfect (VEETARAAG, beyond attachment and aversion). Jains worship quality or merit, not the person. In NAMOKAAR MANTRA, veneration is offered to spiritual-posts such as Arihant, Siddha and Acharya and not to individuals like Mahaveer and Rishabhadev. In the fifth phrase, NAMO LOYE SAVVA SAAHOONAM,[13] the words 'LOYE (world)' and 'SAVVA (all)' demonstrate the tolerance of the Jains. It is not the person but his spiritual attitude that is worshipped. Difference in name is immaterial since every name connotes the same spiritual perfection. Haribhadrasuri says,[14] "I venerate all those who are free from all vices and adorned with all virtues, be they Brahma, Vishnu, Shiva or Jin." Acharya Hemchandra wrote,[15] "I worship those who have destroyed attachment and aversion, the seeds of birth and death, be they Brahma, Vishnu, Shiva or Jin." Pandit Jugal

11 SANMATI PRAKARAN 1/28, Siddhasen Jnanodaya Trust, Ahmedabad, 1963.

12 ADHYAATMOPANISHAT, Shri Jain Dharm Prasarak Sabha, Bhavanagar, Vikram 1965.

13 Reverence to all monks of the world. Reverence to Jain monks only is not offered.

14 LOKATATTVANIRNAYA Jain Granth Prakashak Sabha, Ahmedabad, Vikram 1994.

15 MAHADEV STOTRA, 44, published in PARAMAARTH SWAADHYAAYA GRANTH SAMGRAH.

Kishore Mukhtar, an eminent Jain scholar, reformer and poet, has expressed similar thoughts.[16]

### The Door To Liberation Is Open To All

Jainism holds that followers of any religion can attain perfection or emancipation if they destroy attachment and aversion. The door to salvation is open to all. We do not believe that only the followers of Jainism can achieve emancipation. Haribhadrasuri, a staunch advocate of religious tolerance, remarks,[17] "One who can attain equanimity of mind will for certain get the emancipation whether he is a Shwetambar or Digambar or a Buddhist or any one else."

About the means to liberation as well, the Jains are broad minded. They do not believe that their mode of worship or their religious practices alone represent the way to reach the goal of emancipation. For them, it is not the external modes of worship but the right attitude (rational perception) and mental purity which make religious practices fruitful. The ACHAARAANG SUTRA clearly states the practices that are considered to be the cause of bondage may be the cause of liberation also. It is the intrinsic purity, not the external practices which makes a person religious.[18] Haribhadrasuri propounds that neither one who remains without clothes nor one who wears white clothes, neither a logician nor a metaphysician nor a devotee of a personal cult will get liberation unless he overcomes his passions.[19] If we accept the diversity of modes of worship according to the time, place and levels of aspirants, and emphasize the intrinsic purity in religious matters, then we cannot condemn the religious practices of others as false.

As for scriptures, the Jain outlook is likewise liberal. We believe that an unsound scripture (MITHYA SHRUT) may be a sound scripture (SAMYAK SHRUT) for a person with the right attitude and a sound scripture may turn false for a person with a perverse attitude. It is not the scripture but the attitude of the follower that makes it true or false. It is the vision of the interpreter and practitioner that counts.[20]

---

16 See 'My Aspirations (MERI BHAAVANA)', Studies In Jainism: Reader 1, published by Jain Study Circle, 1990, page 46.

17 JAIN, BUDDHA AUR GITA KA ACHARADARSHAN by Dr. Sagarmal Jain, volume 2, page 5, 1982.

18 Book 1, lecture 4, lesson 2, verse 1.

19 UPADESH TARANGINI, 1/8, page 98, Bhurabhai Harshchandra, Varanasi, Veer Samvat 2437.

20 NANDISUTRA, 72, page 30, Mahavir Jain Vidyalaya, Bombay, 1968.

## References To Religious Tolerance In Jain Literature

In SUTRAKRITAANG, the second earliest Jain scripture (2nd century B.C.), it is stated that those who praise their own faith, disparage their opponents', and possess malice against them will remain confined to the cycle of birth and death.[21]

In SHAASTRAVAARTA SAMUCHCHAYA which is one of the foremost works illustrating Haribhadrasuri's liberal outlook, it is mentioned that the great sage, venerable Bhagwaan Buddha preached the doctrines of momentariness (KSHANIKAVAAD), non-existence of soul (ANAATMAVAAD), idealism (VIJNAANAVAAD) and nothingness (SHOONYAVAAD) solely with the intention to eliminate the 'mineness' and desire for worldly objects. Like a good physician who prescribes medicine according to the disease and nature of the patient, Buddha identified with the level of mental development of his followers.[22] Haribhadrasuri has the same liberal and regardful attitude towards SAMKHYA and NYAAYA schools of Indian philosophy. He maintains that naturalism (PRAKRITIVAAD) of SAMKHYA and creationism (ISHWARA-KARTAAVAAD) of NYAAYA are also true and justified if viewed from a certain standpoint.[23] In the history of world religions, Haribhadrasuri's crusade against sectarianism is unique and admirable.

## Concluding Remarks

It is evident that Jainism has a sound philosophical foundation for religious tolerance. Throughout the ages, it has remained tolerant and regardful of other faiths and ideologies. Jains have neither indulged in aggressive campaigns in the name of religion nor did they invoke divine sanction for cruelties against people of alien faiths. Although, in the Jain literature, religions have been classified as wrong belief (MITHYA DRISHTI) and right belief (SAMYAK DRISHTI), yet wrong belief is defined as possessing a one-sided (absolutist) view while the right

21 Book 1, lecture 1, chapter 2, verse 23.

On many occasions, during Jain worships and celebrations, we recite "PRADHAANAM SARVA DHARMAANAAM" which means that the Jainism is supreme among all religious systems. Sometimes it is implied that being born into a Jain family is the consequence of past beneficial karma. Such slogans and pronouncements do not reflect the basic principles of the Jain religion. They do not conform to our principle of relativism (SYAADAVAAD). Moreover, they may be offensive to the followers of other religions. - D. C. J.

22 SHASTRAVAARTA SAMUCHCHAYA 6/464, 65, 67, L. D. Institute of Indology, Ahmedabad, 1969.

23 ibid 3/207; 3/237.

belief consists in having an unprejudiced view that sees truth in an opponent's beliefs also. Considering Jainism as the confluence of one-sided views,[24] Acharya Siddhasen (5th century A.D.) writes,[25] "Be glorious the teachings of JIN which are the union of all absolutist views – the organic synthesis of one-sided and partial views, the essence of spiritual nectar which is easily understood by the aspirants of salvation."

We Jains believe in the unity of all religions, but unity, according to us, does not imply omnivorous unity in which all religions lose their entity and identity. We believe in the unity in which all religions will join with each other to form an organic whole without losing their own independent existence. In other words, we believe in a harmonious coexistence or a liberal synthesis in which all components maintain their intrinsic features and work for the common goal of peace of mankind. One may raise the slogan of 'one world religion' but, in view of the diversities in human thoughts, it is neither possible nor practicable to have a single religion. Acharya Kundkund has written that there are different individuals having different activities and karma. They have different levels of understanding and capacities. So one should not engage in heated discussions with persons belonging to other sects or those belonging to one's own sect.[26]

Acharya Amitgati (11th century A.D.) beautifully expresses religious tolerance in the following verse:[27]

SATTVESHU MAITRI GUNISHU PRAMODAM
KLISHTESHU JEEVESHU KRIPAAPARATVAM
MAADHYASTHA BHAAVAM VIPAREET VRITTAU
SADA MAMAATMA VIDADHAATU DEVA.

O Bhagwaan, I wish to have friendly feelings for all beings,
delightful respect for the virtuous ones,
utmost compassion for the afflicted beings, and
equanimity towards those whose views are contrary to mine.

---

24 Hinduism consists of a variety of schools of thought. Thus it can be considered a confluence of a number of one-sided views. - D. C. J.

25 SANMATI TARK PRAKARAN, 3/69, Jnaanodaya Trust, Ahmedabad, 1963.

26 NIYAMASAAR, couplet 155, The Central Jaina Publishing House, Lucknow, 1931.

27 SAAMAAYIK PAATH. verse 1, included in Lesson 24, page 78.